The battle of the Boyne 1690

A guide to the battlefield

Harman Murtagh is a recognised expert on Irish military history, particularly the Jacobite War of 1689–1691, on which he has written and lectured extensively throughout Ireland and abroad. He is a vice-president of the Military History Society of Ireland and a former editor of that society's respected journal, *The Irish Sword*. He was historical advisor to the Ulster Museum's *Kings in Conflict* exhibition in 1990, and is currently an advisor to the OPW on the Battle of the Boyne project. He is a senior lecturer in Athlone Institute of Technology.

The battle of the Boyne 1690
A guide to the battlefield

Harman Murtagh

*

PUBLISHED BY
THE BOYNE VALLEY HONEY COMPANY

2006

First published in paperback in 2006 by
The Boyne Valley Honey Company
Mell, Drogheda, County Louth
www.boynevalleyhoney.com

ISBN 0-9517823-3-9
978-0-9517823-3-0

Designed and Typeset in Ireland by Compuscript Ltd.
Maps by Sarah Gearty
Illustrations by Richard Hook
Aerial photography by Esler Crawford at Esler Crawford Photography
Edited by Rachel Pierce at Verba Editing House
Printed in Ireland by BetaPrint Ltd.

Dedication

In memory of Dr J.G. Simms, FTCD,
who first introduced the author to the battlefield of the Boyne.

A note on the Boyne Valley Honey Company

Honey is a very special product. It is the only food we eat today that is produced in exactly the same way as it was thousands of years ago, without anything added to it, or taken from it. It is because it is so special that we like to associate it with unique and worthwhile promotions, one of the most important of these being publishing books that preserve and record Irish history, heritage and culture. *The Battle of the Boyne 1690, A Guide to the Battlefield* is just such a book. It gives us at the Boyne Valley Honey Company great pleasure to be associated with this publication.

If you are interested in other Boyne Valley Honey publications, please visit our website at www.boynevalleyhoney.com

Other publications include:

In Praise of Honey, Charlton & Newdick
Irish High Crosses, Peter Harbison
Treasures of the Boyne Valley, Peter Harbison
Treasures from the National Library of Ireland, ed. Noel Kissane
Treasures from the National Museum of Ireland, ed. Patrick F. Wallace
The Battle of the Boyne 1690: The Drummer Boy's Story, Brenda Maguire
The Boyne Valley book and tape of Irish Legends, Brenda Maguire

Acknowledgements

The idea for this book and much of the drive for its publication comes from Malachy McCloskey, Managing Director of the Boyne Valley Honey Company of Drogheda, its publishers. The author is most grateful for his encouragement and enthusiasm for the project at all stages of its production. The author has also benefited greatly from the insights and professional military analysis of Colonel Donal O'Carroll, president of the Military History Society of Ireland. He also acknowledges his debt to Ms Rachel Pierce of Verba Editing House, Drogheda, for skill and commitment, as Managing Editor, in bringing the book to publication. Special thanks are due to Richard Hook, illustrator, for his vibrant and convincing illustrations of the action at certain key moments in the battle, and also to Esler Crawford for a most enjoyable day spent photographing the Boyne Valley from above.

Picture credits

Contents

Foreword

The Battle of the Boyne would surely make one believe in guardian angels, for how otherwise would William of Orange have survived it after at least two attempts on his life – and the potential threat of another? By snatching victory from the jaws of death, he not only won the battle but ensured that his success would alter the balance of power in Europe and change the whole history of Ireland for centuries to come. How fate hangs from a very slender thread, and how the course of Irish and European history might have been very different had William succumbed to any one of those attacks? But the fact is that he did survive – and consequently romped home the winner of the only European campaign that was ever fought on Irish soil.

He may not have been a great general himself or had great ones to guide him, but he was a shrewder and a better fighter than his Stuart opponent and father-in-law, James II, who only cared for the Irish when they supported him and then became ungracious about them when his lack of leadership lost the war for him – and them. It is no wonder that many Irish remember him more by a faecal epithet than as a supporter of the Catholic cause.

Harman Murtagh gives a very honest pen picture of the two kings and other major participants in this battle, providing a frank assessment of the strengths and weaknesses of their respective characters. He looks at the contest with the trained and unbiased eye of the military historian, stepping worthily into the shoes of his mentor, Gerald Simms, to whom the book is dedicated. With a tactician's insight, he studies the ebb and flow of the Boyne and the course of events on both banks of that fateful river, bringing us through them step by step from the crucial vantage points of the contest. In preparing us for the heat of battle (which, as he says, must have been terrifying for those in the thick of it), he provides us with some fascinating insights into warfare at the time, such as the dangers inherent in firing a matchlock musket, which required forty-four separate movements, and that oboes were used to communicate orders to dragoons on the field of battle.

Harman Murtagh's text is neatly complemented by the illustrations specially commissioned from Richard Hook for this volume. These help to waft us back to 1690 to participate in the atmosphere of frenetic activity as thousands of men on foot or on horseback faced each other in hand-to-hand combat. Sarah Gearty's maps, and most notably that in the foldout at the back of the book, lead us through the highways and by-ways of the terrain and illuminate the location of the aerial photographs specially taken by Esler Crawford that give us, literally, a bird's-eye view of the battlefield, which has changed comparatively little in the 316 years since hostilities began and ended.

Finally, compliments are due to Malachy McCloskey of Boyne Valley Honey Company, whose own interest and research into seventeenth-century Irish history led him intuitively to choose the battle of the Boyne as the subject of his latest title in his series of publications which, I am proud to say, includes two of my own books, listed on page vi. This volume by Harman can only serve to immerse him even more deeply in the period, and provide us all with a user-friendly guide to one of the most cataclysmic events in Irish history, the wounds from which will hopefully soon be forgotten so as to allow us all live peacefully together on this lovely little island of ours.

Peter Harbison
Loughshinny

Preface

The author of this guidebook to the battle of the Boyne, which he rightly calls the most famous military engagement in Irish history, needs no recommendation from me. Let readers judge for themselves how well he performs the historian's task of exploring and explaining the events of that day in July 1690. I am nevertheless delighted to have this opportunity of setting down – and in a publication so attractive and so likely to reach a large public – my high opinion of Harman Murtagh and his work.

Our acquaintance goes back a long way. To the best of my recollection, we first met on another Irish battlefield, the one near Benburb in County Armagh where the army of Owen Roe O'Neill won a remarkable victory over the Scottish Covenanters of General Monro in 1646. Like Benburb and the Boyne, that outing of the Military History Society of Ireland took place on a hot summer day – so hot indeed that even just walking the ground at Drumflugh, unencumbered by arms and armour, was memorably uncomfortable. The leader of the expedition, Professor Hayes-McCoy, then in his prime, gave a lively exposition of the battle, after which we were all revived by the timely hospitality of the priory at Benburb. It was a memorable occasion.

Since that time, Harman has added to his reputation as a highly regarded military historian. He has been editor of *The Irish Sword* (the journal of the Military History Society of Ireland) over a long period; he is a prolific author and indispensable contributor to many publications; and is also a stimulating lecturer on the 1600–1800 period in particular. When my colleagues and I at the Ulster Museum were working on the Boyne tercentenary exhibition, his enthusiastic support was helpful and reassuring. (I should perhaps explain that initially the very idea of tackling the subject of the Boyne was regarded at the time with some trepidation.) He also contributed a chapter to the book of essays produced to accompany the show. Also notable was the lecture he gave to a large and keenly interested audience in Belfast City Hall. (The City Council sponsored a whole series of lectures on the same general theme and on a higher scale of municipal munificence altogether, the Council paid the whole cost of a really splendid exhibition catalogue.) Anyhow, the councillor whose duty it was to move the vote of thanks on this occasion congratulated Harman on his excellent performance and said he had greatly enjoyed it but, unable to let the truth remain unheard, he added: 'Of course, I know what really happened, and I know I'm right'.

A parting shot, so to speak. Students of history are sometimes tempted to wonder how things might have turned out if some turning point had been different. These 'What if?' questions are generally pretty futile for any serious purpose, but they can remind us that what actually happened was not inevitable until it happened. The Boyne is one of the best exercises for such a subject, with two kings leading their armies in person and with important consequences for whichever won or lost. The Williamite historian, George Story, who was there himself, wondered what would have happened if the Jacobite cannon ball that had injured William the day before had killed him. He concluded that whatever the effect on the future, 'it would have been of fatal consequence to the army at the time, if he had fallen, since instead of our going to them, the Irish would have been ready to come to us next morning, and how we would have received them there's none can tell.'

To the author, congratulations and best wishes. To all concerned in the production of this guide, may all your hopes for its success be fulfilled and to all who seek to understand the battle and to find answers to their questions with the help of it, have a good day out.

W.A. Maguire
Institute of Irish Studies
Queen's University, Belfast

Introduction

The battle of the Boyne, fought in 1690, is the most famous military engagement in Irish history. The armies of the rival kings – James II and William III – which numbered between them more than 60,000 men, were by far the largest forces ever assembled on an Irish battlefield. The soldiers were of many different nationalities, about one third being Irish. Both James and William claimed the crowns of England, Ireland and Scotland, therefore much was at stake when they faced one another across the River Boyne on 1 July 1690. William was, in addition, *stadholder* (effectively leader and military commander) of the Dutch Republic, while James had the active support of King Louis XIV of France, Europe's most powerful sovereign. The generals who directed operations on the battlefield were largely European professional soldiers – French, Dutch, German, British and Irish – in the service of one or other of the three kings.

These facts indicate that the battle of the Boyne was an event of European importance. James's defeat secured William's position on the British throne and was a setback for Louis. It was significant in the history of Ireland because it was an important milestone in the ultimate Williamite victory, which consolidated Protestant/new-settler ascendancy and ended any possibility of a recovery of economic and political power by the older Catholic *élites*, Gaelic and Anglo-Norman. Despite its great impact in socio-political terms, in purely military terms the Boyne was a relatively tame engagement: neither army was fully engaged and casualties were light.

There are many eyewitness accounts of the battle from officers and spectators on both sides, and at least one contemporary map. These sources provide us with much information on the concepts, planning and details of what occurred and give a good idea of the timing, scale and significance of the major troop dispositions and movements. The Dutch artist, Dirk Maas, was present at the battlefield. His paintings and engraving of the action at Oldbridge are an important visual record and the progenitor of several well-known paintings by his contemporary and fellow-countryman, Jan Wyck. Many other engravings and prints depicting the battle or important moments of it – such as the symbolic image of William in heroic posture crossing the river – are purely imaginative and were published for propaganda purposes.

The battle of the Boyne has attracted the attention of numerous scholars and soldier-scholars. It has been the subject of several books, articles and

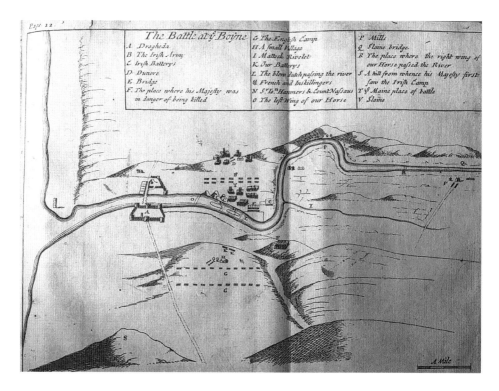

George Story's contemporary map

television programmes. In 1990 the Ulster Museum in Belfast staged a splendid exhibition to commemorate its tercentenary, accompanied by a fine catalogue that is a mine of information and illustrations. A significant portion of the battle site is owned by the Irish government, which has established an interpretative centre at Oldbridge House. Preliminary archaeological investigation in the area has revealed the exact site of Oldbridge village and other information.

This publication differs from previous writings on the Boyne in an important respect. It is intended as a handy pocket-guide which, after filling in the general background and describing the issues, forces and leading personalities involved, takes the visitor round the battlefield to a number of strategic viewing points. At each location a description and analysis of what took place is offered. Topography played a major part in determining the course of the battle of the Boyne, and the relative absence of urbanisation makes it possible to relate satisfactorily the events of more than 300 years ago to the modern landscape. For this purpose, the maps provided identify the decisive manoeuvres at key moments of the battle. Other illustrations attempt to convey a sense of the actuality of seventeenth-century warfare and of the drama of the contest at the Boyne. It is hoped that this guide will help the visitor to have an enjoyable and informative day on the battlefield, and to leave it with a deeper understanding of the many facets of an engagement that had repercussions not only in Ireland and Britain but throughout Europe.

Harman Murtagh, 2006

Battle of the Boyne 1690 by Jan Wyck

A divided Europe

The battle of the Boyne is the most famous event in the major war that engulfed Ireland between 1689 and 1691. Three related factors lay behind the conflict: the Glorious Revolution, King Louis XIV's response to it and the ongoing struggle between Catholics and Protestants for land and power in Ireland.

In Irish the war is called *cogadh an dá rí*, or 'the war of the two kings', from its most obvious cause: the attempt by the deposed King James II to recover the throne of England, which he had lost in 1688 to his Dutch son-in-law, William of Orange, now

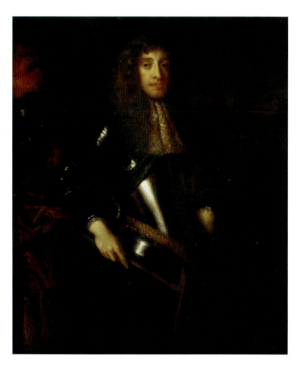

King James II

crowned King William III as joint sovereign with his wife, Mary, who was James's daughter. As a zealous Roman Catholic convert, James had been in an uncomfortable position as sovereign of a largely Protestant people, and his difficulties were compounded by his poor political sense. The birth of his son, James Francis Edward, in 1688 promised a Catholic succession,

King William III

which in turn triggered William's invasion of England and seizure of power.

This 'Glorious Revolution' (so-called because it effected the change of regime with a minimum of violence) enjoyed considerable public support in England, at least amongst the political classes. The reaction in Scotland was mixed, however, and in Ireland the majority Catholic population remained strongly loyal to James. The situation was sufficiently fluid for a restoration of the deposed king to remain a distinct possibility, and in March 1689 James landed in Kinsale, hoping to use Ireland as a stepping-stone towards the recovery of his English throne. William, for his part, needed a comprehensive victory over James not only to secure Ireland and consolidate his British regime but to preserve his prestige in Europe.

Modern historians sometimes refer to the conflict as the war of the three kings because it made Ireland an important theatre in the wider international struggle between King Louis XIV of France and a Grand Alliance of European powers in which William was one of the principal leaders. Since the French invasion of The Netherlands in the 1670s, William's public life had been devoted to opposing Louis, the most powerful sovereign in Europe, who had a record of international aggression. Besides Protestant states, William's allies included several Catholic princes: the Holy Roman emperor, the king of Spain and the elector of Bavaria. Pope Innocent XI, who had quarrelled with Louis, was also sympathetic, although after his death in 1689 his successor, Alexander VIII, was more disposed to be neutral. In the late 1680s an international war was therefore imminent. William's seizure of England was prompted by the need to add her burgeoning economic and military power to the anti-French alliance. The Glorious Revolution took Louis by surprise and represented a frustrating setback to his plans.

King Louis XIV

The Grand Alliance and its allies against France ---

Holy Roman Emperor
Dutch Republic
England
Spain and Spanish Netherlands
Denmark
Savoy
Brandenburg
Bavaria
Saxony
Lorraine
Lesser German states

The second factor that led to war was Louis's countermove, intended to destabilise William's new regime by backing James's restoration. Clearly, if this strategy proved successful, William would be weakened and England would become the ally of France. At the very least, James's presence at the head of an army in Ireland would distract William's attention and resources

A French view of James II's journey to Ireland

'I have an idea that when a man plays his last stake, he ought to play it himself or to be on the spot. The king of England seems to be in this condition. His last stake is Ireland; it appears to me that he ought to go there, where with the help, which the king [of France] may give him, he can get on his legs again and be supported by those of his subjects who remain loyal to him.'

- Marshal Vauban

from the principal theatre of military operations on the Continent. So it was that French ships carried James to Ireland in 1689, with Louis's blessing. Furthermore, between then and 1691 the Irish Jacobite army was sustained by French personnel, munitions and money. The French intervention had the immediate consequence of bringing England into the alliance against France. This fulfilled William's major objective, but he would probably have engineered it in any case.

Ireland before the battle

In Ireland, a century of adversity before the battle of the Boyne had largely united Roman Catholics of both Gaelic-Irish and Anglo-Norman ancestry. They formed about three quarters of the estimated total population of 2.2 million, but through conquest and plantation had lost heavily in wealth and influence to the remaining one quarter: the Protestant immigrants from England and Scotland and their descendants. Led by Richard Talbot, earl (later duke) of Tyrconnell, whom James had appointed to head the Irish government, the Catholics had recovered much of their former political and military power and once again enjoyed freedom to practice their religion. Their outstanding demand was to recover the lands they had lost in the Cromwellian/post-Restoration land settlement.

This concession was politically difficult for James, but when he arrived in Ireland it was made clear to him that it was an essential precondition of Irish Catholic support for his cause. He was forced to summon a parliament, in which the land settlement was reversed in favour of the Catholics and several thousand of the most prominent Irish Protestants were outlawed because they supported William. The third issue in the war, therefore, was the struggle for supremacy in Ireland between the older Catholic inhabitants and the newer Protestant settlers. Each group sought ascendancy through its respective support for James and William. James's supporters are called Jacobites from *Jacobus*, the Latin version of his name; William's supporters are known simply as Williamites.

The government of Ireland

Late seventeenth-century Ireland, like Scotland, was a separate kingdom, with its own legal system, army and occasional parliament. It was not independent, however. The king of England was always its king and closely controlled the Irish government through a residential chief governor – the lord lieutenant, lord deputy or chief justices – on whom he also relied for advice. One of Tyrconnell's great political strengths was the extent of his influence with James II. All bills brought before an Irish parliament required prior royal approval. On this and other matters relating to Ireland, the king was counselled by his English ministers (just as in military matters he was advised by his generals), but the ultimate decisions remained his. While the system was not democratic, it was politically advisable for the king to take into account the opinion of the political and tax-paying class, especially in times of crisis. James II's reluctance to do so was a prime cause of his political downfall in England. In Ireland, his political weakness compelled him to be more amenable to the views of Tyrconnell and the Irish Catholics. William III was by inclination no less authoritarian than James, but the fact that he had been conferred with his crown by the English parliament, coupled with his wartime taxation needs, ensured that his reign marked a permanent shift in power, in both kingdoms, from the monarchy to parliament.

William was slow to deal with Ireland in 1689, when an early show of force might have brought Tyrconnell's submission. Instead, it was Louis who took the initiative and persuaded the Irish Catholics to resist. Support for William was crushed throughout Ireland, except in west Ulster, where the Protestants of Derry and Enniskillen mounted an effective resistance throughout the summer of 1689. William eventually sent forces to assist them.

The Jacobites were driven out of Ulster by these combined forces, and in August a substantial Williamite army, commanded by the elderly Marshal Schomberg, landed near Belfast and marched south towards Dublin. The offensive came to a halt at Dundalk, where the army was confronted by a Jacobite force under James's command. Both sides were about 20,000-strong. Schomberg was over-cautious, his troops were mostly inexperienced and his transport, supply, artillery and medical services deficient. When disease broke out among his men, he withdrew to winter quarters in Ulster, leaving the other provinces to the Jacobites.

William had placed great trust in Schomberg, who had an international military reputation. He was therefore deeply disappointed by Schomberg's failure to secure a speedy victory. In the face of this unexpected setback,

---
The different Irish factions

Broadly speaking, Irish Catholics supported James II while Irish Protestants backed William. Neither group was entirely homogeneous, however. On the Catholic side, those of Norman ancestry – the Old English – took the lead, with the descendants of the Gaels in a subordinate role, albeit not always contentedly. In the wake of military setbacks, further divisions developed between those loyal to James and a more nationalist faction, while a 'new interest' group of recent land-purchasers actively favoured peace. Protestants were sharply divided between Anglicans, who were of English origin, and Presbyterians, whose background was Scottish and who were generally less wealthy and more outspoken. An Anglican minority (its size is debated) had a conscientious objection to James's deposition, and in varying degrees withheld its support from William.

William resolved to campaign in Ireland himself in the summer of 1690. His army was greatly strengthened beforehand by veterans brought in from the Continent, and he took care to address the many deficiencies of organisation that had hindered Schomberg. He landed in Ulster in mid-June and a week later took the offensive at the head of 36,000 men, marching south towards Dublin.

The Jacobite side was reinforced by the arrival of a brigade of French infantry. The French advice was to abandon Dublin and the provinces of Leinster and Munster. However, it would have been a huge political embarrassment for James to have withdrawn from this rich territory without a fight. Accordingly, he marched north with 25,000 men to confront William. After a skirmish at the Moyry Pass (between Dundalk and Newry), the Jacobite army withdrew to a position immediately west of Drogheda, on the south bank of the River Boyne. The river formed the last remaining defensible physical obstacle between William and Dublin. William and his army followed James south, and on 30 June 1690 pitched camp north of the river, on the high ground at Tullyallen.

Chronology of Events

1685	Accession of James II.
1686	Tyrconnell appointed to command Irish army.
1687	Tyrconnell appointed Irish lord deputy.
1688	Birth of prince of Wales (10 June).
	Louis XIV commences Continental war with invasion of Rhineland (September).
	William of Orange invades England, deposing James II (November).
	James II takes refuge in France (December).
1689	William accepts English crown as joint sovereign with his wife, Mary (13 February).
	James II lands in Ireland (12 March).
	Grand Alliance formed (2 May).
	England declares war on France (7 May).
	Jacobite siege of Derry fails (18 April –31 July).
	Jacobite parliament (7 May–18 July).
	Schomberg lands in Ulster (13 August).
	Schomberg retreats from Dundalk (20 October).
1690	French brigade arrives in Ireland (12 March), in exchange for Irish brigade sent to France.
	William III lands at Carrickfergus (14 June).
	Battle of the Boyne (1 July).
	James II leaves Ireland to return to France (4 July).
	William III enters Dublin (6 July).
	Williamite siege of Limerick fails (9–31 August).
	William III returns to England (5 September).
	Cork surrenders to Marlborough (28 September).
1691	Ginkel takes Athlone for the Williamites (30 June).
	Ginkel heavily defeats Jacobite army under St Ruth at battle of Aughrim (12 July).
	Galway capitulates to Williamites (21 July).
	Second Williamite siege of Limerick commences (25 August).
	Treaty of Limerick signed, ending war in Ireland (3 October).
	12,000 Irish soldiers sail with Sarsfield to France (December).
1695	Irish parliament resumes enactment of anti-Catholic laws.
1697	Treaty of Ryswick ends war on Continent.
1701	James II dies; Louis XIV recognises his son (the 'Old Pretender') as James III.
1702	William III dies, and is succeeded by Queen Anne, James II's daughter.
1715	Louis XIV dies.

PART 2

Some leading personalities

In the late seventeenth century more efficient taxation, enlarged bureaucracies and standing armies empowered kings to exercise the great authority they possessed in law. This was especially true of Louis XIV in France; James II and William III were thwarted from achieving the same level of absolutism by the strength of the political classes in England and in the Dutch Republic, respectively. The personalities and abilities of the kings who wielded such power were important, as were those of the generals to whom they entrusted military command.

This was the situation at the battle of the Boyne, where both James and William played a major role in the conduct of operations, while Louis XIV and his war minister, Louvois, influenced strategy from afar. The strengths and shortcomings of the subordinate generals on either side were also important: they provided professional advice to the kings and, in the absence of modern communications, played a large part in determining the course and outcome of operations in the sectors of the battlefield for which they bore responsibility.

The three kings

William III (1650–1702), king of England and *stadholder* of the Dutch Republic, was Dutch but held a French title (prince of Orange) and had an English mother and wife, respectively James II's sister and daughter, both named Mary. William was an able statesman, whose public life was driven by his distrust of Louis XIV. His military and diplomatic skills were devoted to preserving the Dutch Republic, and Europe in general, from French dominance.

His appearance was unprepossessing: small, thin, hook-nosed and stooped, with the hacking cough of a chronic asthmatic. In personality he was reserved, secretive and taciturn. Although a Calvinist, the necessity to secure Catholic allies against Louis ensured he was not a bigot. He loved hunting and was interested in gardening. He had great personal courage and was at home, and indeed happy, on a battlefield. He was an indifferent general, however, and his battle planning was mediocre and frequently fumbled in its execution.

James II (1633–1701), 'late' king of England, was William's uncle and father-in-law. His conversion to Catholicism in middle age rendered him suspect to his British Protestant subjects, and he displayed stunning political ineptitude in handling their sensitivities after his accession to the throne in 1685. While he was honest and conscientious, he was also stubborn and authoritarian. He was addicted to fox-hunting and was physically energetic and very fit. He enjoyed robust health, apart from a disposition to uncontrollable nosebleeds at times of stress. Above middle height and graceful in appearance and manner, in his younger days he had been a noted womaniser.

Much of his life had been spent with soldiers and sailors, and he shared their simple concept of devotion to duty. He was personally brave and understood military matters, although there is no evidence that he had any gifts as a strategist, or that he was even a competent general. Increasingly, his relationship with his Irish supporters was one of mutual disenchantment. Adversity had made him fatalistic, and by 1690 he had probably little heart for war with William nor any real expectation of military victory.

Louis XIV (1638–1715), king of France, ruled the most populous, prosperous and sophisticated state in Europe. Able, proud and authoritarian, his aggressive foreign policy alarmed his neighbours, and plunged France into war for much of his long personal reign (1661–1715). This brought him into conflict with William, which in turn led to French involvement in Ireland. His support for James's restoration was sincere. Although not personally present at the Boyne, his material support was vital to the Jacobites. Amongst his other achievements, he laid the foundation of the modern French state. In this, he was aided by a number of able administrators, including the marquis de Louvois, France's war minister, who was opposed to military operations overseas, and his rival, the marquis de Seignelay, navy minister and keen supporter of French intervention in Ireland.

Duke of Schomberg

The Williamite generals

Marshal Schomberg (1615–1690), who held the rank of captain general, was an accomplished mercenary soldier of German birth and had served in Germany, Holland, France, England and Portugal. Although a marshal of France, as a devout Protestant he left the service of Louis XIV in 1686 following the revocation the previous year of the edict of Nantes, which had guaranteed Protestant liberties. He played a leading role in William's invasion of England in 1688. He was sent to Ireland in 1689 with a largely new-raised force and inadequate support. His excessive caution and inability to adapt to Irish conditions turned his offensive against James at Dundalk into a fiasco. William was greatly displeased with this, and when he came to Ireland he treated Schomberg with marked disfavour. Although certainly well past his best, Schomberg remained the ablest and most experienced commander in William's army and was retained as captain general, under William, for the Boyne campaign.

The duke of Würtemburg-Neustadt (1659–1701), a German professional soldier in the Danish service, he was the commander of the Danish contingent in William's army, with the rank of lieutenant general, which he had achieved at the age of twenty-three. He had considerable combat experience, having served with distinction in several European campaigns, including the famous relief of Vienna from the Turks in 1683. Noted for his good humour, he was a brave and competent commander.

Duke of Würtemburg-Neustadt

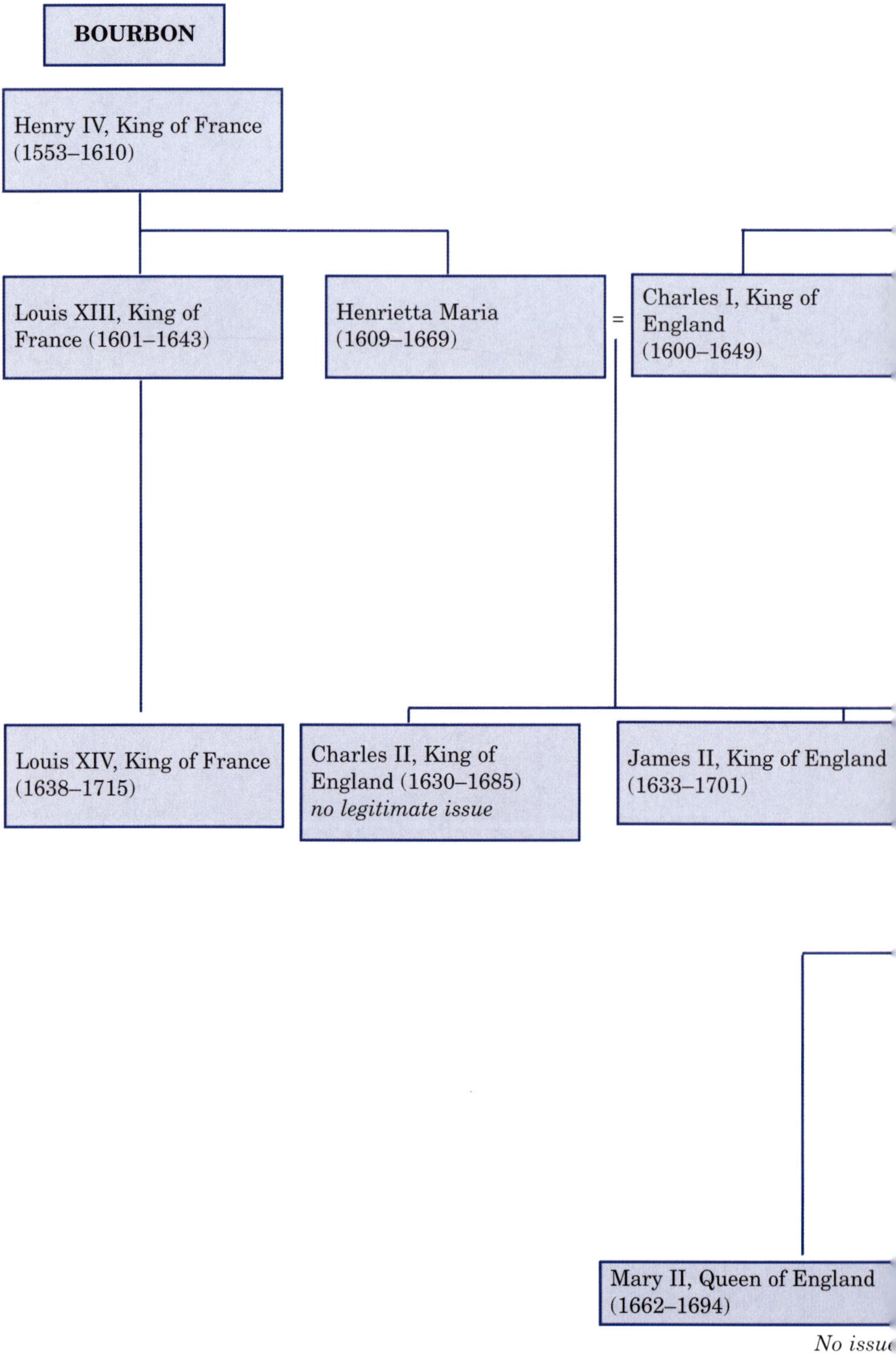

BOURBON

Henry IV, King of France
(1553–1610)

Louis XIII, King of
France (1601–1643)

Henrietta Maria
(1609–1669)

=

Charles I, King of
England
(1600–1649)

Louis XIV, King of France
(1638–1715)

Charles II, King of
England (1630–1685)
no legitimate issue

James II, King of England
(1633–1701)

Mary II, Queen of England
(1662–1694)

No issue

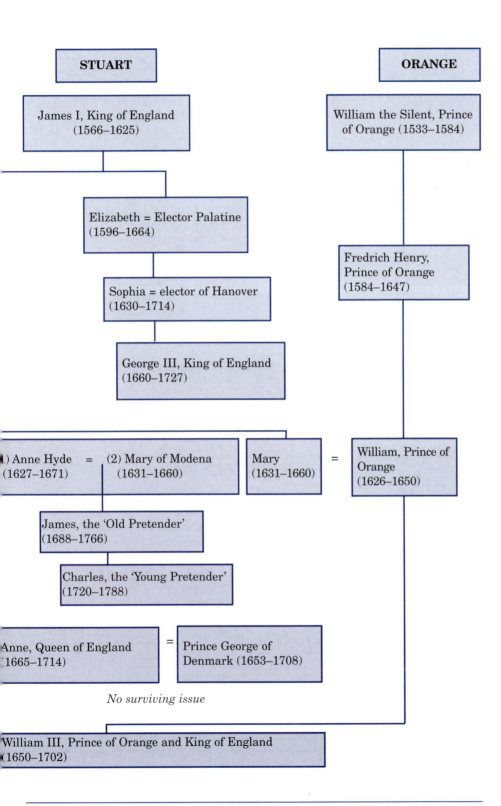

STUART

ORANGE

James I, King of England
(1566–1625)

William the Silent, Prince
of Orange (1533–1584)

Elizabeth = Elector Palatine
(1596–1664)

Fredrich Henry,
Prince of Orange
(1584–1647)

Sophia = elector of Hanover
(1630–1714)

George III, King of England
(1660–1727)

1) Anne Hyde   =   (2) Mary of Modena
(1627–1671)   (1631–1660)

Mary
(1631–1660)

=

William, Prince of
Orange
(1626–1650)

James, the 'Old Pretender'
(1688–1766)

Charles, the 'Young Pretender'
(1720–1788)

Anne, Queen of England
(1665–1714)

=

Prince George of
Denmark (1653–1708)

No surviving issue

William III, Prince of Orange and King of England
(1650–1702)

Count Solms (1636–1693), a Dutch kinsman of William III and commander of the brigade of Dutch footguards, was general of infantry. 'Proud, haughty and not very bright', his dour arrogance and punctilio made him increasingly unpopular with the English section of the army, whose language he could not speak. In battle, however, he was courageous and dogged – qualities William admired. Nonetheless, a general's rank probably exceeded his capability.

Meinhard Schomberg (1641–1719), third son of the marshal, was a German-born mercenary soldier who had served in Portugal, France, Germany and with the imperial forces

Meinhard Schomberg

against the Turks. He was appointed general of cavalry for the 1690 campaign in Ireland. Notoriously harsh and quarrelsome in temperament, he was described as 'one of the hottest, fiery men in England'. His later military career proved undistinguished and he retired to civilian life, reportedly having 'quarrelled with everybody except the enemy'.

James Douglas (d. 1691), younger son of a Scottish peer and a strong Protestant, was the commander of the small Scottish army before the revolution of 1688, at which time he defected to William III. He was the senior British officer at the Boyne, with the rank of lieutenant general. He was quarrelsome, lacked combat experience and displayed little natural command ability when given his opportunity in Ireland.

James Douglas

Duke of Tyrconnell

The Jacobite generals

The duke of Tyrconnell (1630–1691), from a cadet branch of the Talbots of Malahide, was the principal spokesman of the Irish Catholics and a close *confidant* of James II, who gave him command of the Irish army on his accession and in 1687 made him viceroy of Ireland. The Irish army was largely Tyrconnell's creation, and he held the senior rank of captain general. As such, he commanded the right wing of the army at the Boyne. Although he participated fully in the formation of Jacobite strategy, he was a tough and able politician rather than a soldier, and probably depended on military professionals for tactical battlefield advice.

The comte de Lauzun (1632–1723), a precocious French courtier, commanded the French brigade in Ireland in 1690 with the rank of captain general. He had no command experience but was a favourite of James II, who had secured his appointment and valued his advice. Few others, however, French or Irish, held any confidence in him, and if he did not behave as badly as predicted, he certainly added nothing to the Jacobite military leadership. Fearful of Louvois, the French war minister, Lauzun thought only of preserving his force, which consequently contributed much less to the war effort than expected.

His fear of Louvois dated back to his confinement in the military prison of Pignerol, the penalty he incurred for his proposal of marriage to Mlle de

Comte de Lauzun

Montpensier, Louis XIV's first cousin, which the king regarded as a personal affront. After ten years, when she purchased his freedom, they were reunited and perhaps secretly married, only to quarrel and separate again within a short time.

The duke of Berwick (1670–1734), an illegitimate son of James II, returned from a military career on the Continent to support his father's cause. He was a courageous and able soldier, later becoming a marshal of France. In Ireland he displayed plenty of energy and leadership ability, but his youth and comparative inexperience suggest his appointment to the rank of lieutenant general was premature.

Duke of Berwick

Richard Hamilton (d. 1717), a brother-in-law of Tyrconnell's wife, was an experienced Irish professional soldier who had served in France. He had been a general in England in 1688 and held the rank of lieutenant general at the Boyne, where he was second-in-command to Tyrconnell on the right wing. He was witty, brave and energetic, but the French had little confidence in his military ability following his failure to capture Derry in 1689. However, this negative opinion may have been coloured by indiscreet advances made by Hamilton to the princess de Conti, a daughter of Louis XIV, for which he had earlier been banished from the French court.

The marquis de Léry-Girardin (d. 1699), an able French cavalry officer, had come to Ireland in 1689 and held the rank of lieutenant general in the Irish army. Unusually for a French officer, he was reluctant to leave Ireland when ordered to accompany James II to France.

The marquis de La Hoguette (d. 1693) was second-in-command of the French expeditionary force sent to Ireland in 1690. He was a professional soldier of ability and a protégé of Louvois, to whom he reported regularly, sometimes in cipher. He was critical of Lauzun, and had contempt for the Irish, urging the evacuation of the French from Ireland after the Boyne.

Dominic Sheldon (d. 1721), an English Catholic career soldier with extensive continental military experience, had served in the Irish army under Tyrconnell. At the Boyne he held the rank of lieutenant general of cavalry and served with courage on the embattled Jacobite right wing.

Patrick Sarsfield (1655–1693) was primarily a cavalryman, and in 1690 held the rank of major general. As a young officer he had served on the Continent and in England, before returning to a command in Ireland in 1689. Immensely tall and striking in appearance, his flair and ability soon marked him out as the out-

Patrick Sarsfield

standing Irish soldier of the war. He earned fame in the autumn of 1690 for his daring destruction of the Williamite artillery train at Ballyneety, and thereafter was the inspiration of the stubborn Irish defence of the line of the Shannon, for which he was created earl of Lucan, the village near Dublin that was the location of his family estate. At the Boyne he was posted on the Jacobite left wing and played only a minor role in the battle.

The armies and their weapons

The Jacobite army that contested the Boyne comprised about 25,000 soldiers, 1,300 of whom garrisoned Drogheda. Almost half the available infantry was absent from the battle because it was deployed on garrison duty in the south and west of Ireland. The core of the army was the small, pre-war Irish standing army, supplemented by a large number of new troops raised by Tyrconnell in 1689 and a 6,500-strong brigade of French infantry sent by Louis XIV in 1690. Most of the Jacobite officers were Irish, as were almost all the non-commissioned officers and ordinary soldiers. The majority were new to soldiering and only a very few had pre-war combat experience. At first, Tyrconnell's preference was to commission Catholics of Anglo-Norman ancestry, like himself, but the expansion of the army forced him to employ large numbers of Gaelic Irish. Some English and Scottish Catholics held commissions, and many regiments had at least one French officer with modern military expertise. Of the six French regiments, one consisted of Walloons and another was largely comprised of Germans, many of whom were Protestants. The generals who commanded the Jacobite army at the Boyne were French, Irish, English and Scottish.

The Jacobite army at the Boyne

9 cavalry regiments
7 dragoon regiments
26 Irish infantry battalions
7 French infantry battalions
16-gun field-artillery train
Total: about 25,000 men

William III's army had been built up to 36,000. It was a very cosmopolitan force and included significant contingents of Dutch, English, Danes, Huguenots and Ulster Protestants. The Continental soldiers were regarded as experienced professionals, whereas the English lacked military experience and were therefore more equivalent to their Irish opponents. William's Ulstermen were rough and disorderly but fought with courage and enthusiasm. Some of the Dutch, recruited in the southern provinces of The Netherlands, were Catholics. William's generals presented an impressive array of European professional soldiers; none was Irish, and of fourteen above the rank of brigadier, only three were British.

Dutch pikeman and sergeant

The Williamite army at the Boyne
---

23 cavalry regiments
5 dragoon regiments
38 infantry battalions
40-gun field-artillery train
6 howitzers
Total: about 36,000 men

The organisation, weaponry and appearance of both armies was much the same. The bulk of the troops were infantry, organised in single-battalion regiments, each named after its colonel, typically either a professional soldier or, in Britain and Ireland, a wealthy, often titled, amateur. Each regiment was subdivided into thirteen companies, with a nominal strength of fifty men and commanded by a captain, lieutenant and ensign. French regiments were somewhat larger, with sixteen companies, and often comprised more than one battalion. King William's Dutch footguards made three battalions; King James's Irish footguards made two.

The principal weapon of the ordinary soldier was a matchlock musket, although some, especially on the Williamite side, were equipped with more modern flintlocks. When fully equipped each soldier would also have had a sword, although these were in short supply. Infantry battalions marched in columns, but deployed into six files on the battlefield. This allowed the regiment to fire two musket volleys in quick succession, one from the foremost three files, which then deployed to the rear to reload, allowing the second three files to discharge a second volley. The effective range for musket shot was about 100m. The black powder used as the explosive agent generated vast amounts of sulphurous smoke, making it a considerable advantage to have the wind blowing into the faces of the enemy. It was also an advantage to have the sun behind an army, so as to impede the vision of its opponents. These simple but important effects are easily forgotten because they are so irrelevant in modern warfare.

A matchlock musket

Irish footguards musketeer

Musketeer of earl of Antrim's regiment

The firing procedure for a matchlock musket was complex and required forty-four separate movements. To load, a musketeer took a pre-prepared charge of powder from a bandolier (a belt with twelve containers, each with sufficient powder for one shot), which he wore across his left shoulder, and poured it down the barrel. He followed this with a lead musket ball from his pouch and a paper wad, all of which he rammed home with a wooden ramrod. He next poured priming powder from his powder flask into the pan, and then, to obtain a spark, blew on the end of a slow-burning match of flax or hemp, which he attached to a hammer. Presenting his weapon towards the target, he pulled the trigger, which depressed the hammer, causing the spark to ignite the powder in the pan. The flash passed through a small touch-hole in the side of the breach to ignite the main charge of powder inside the barrel, which in turn discharged the musket ball. There was a high chance of a misfire from damp match or powder, the latter often producing 'a flash in the pan', whereby the powder in the pan failed to ignite that in the barrel. Firing a matchlock musket placed a soldier in considerable risk of injury.

The newer flintlock muskets were safer and more reliable. Instead of relying on a smouldering match, they were fired by sparking flint on steel. Generally, to avoid bruising, or even dislocation of the shoulder from its

A flintlock carbine

severe 'kick', the musket butt was tucked under the armpit. Pistols and car-bines, which were the shorter muskets carried by dragoons, were loaded and fired in the same way as flintlock muskets.

Once their muskets had been discharged, the soldiers became vulnerable to attack. To protect them, each company had a quota of pikemen. The Williamites were in the process of being equipped with bayonets, which made a pikeman out of every musketeer. Several of their battalions, including the Huguenots and some of the Danes, were caught in the transition: without pikes or bayonets, they were extremely vulnerable to cavalry attack. Battalions sometimes defended themselves with a line of sharp poles stuck into the ground, or portable barricades called *chevaux-de-frise*. Otherwise, their only defence after firing a shot was 'club-musket' – the rather *ad hoc* solution of holding a weapon by its barrel and swinging its butt as a club. Each battalion had a company of grenadiers that formed the vanguard in any attack and was armed with hand grenades and axes, as well as muskets.

Military ranks

general officers:
captain general
lieutenant general
major general
brigadier

regimental officers:
colonel
lieutenant colonel
major
captain
lieutenant
ensign/cornet
quartermaster
adjutant/surgeon/chaplain

other ranks:
sergeant
corporal
drummer/trumpeter
private

Pikeman of Lord Louth's regiment

Irish footguards grenadier

About one quarter of each army comprised mounted soldiers, that is cavalry and dragoons. The cavalry was armed with sabres and pistols. It was organised in regiments, subdivided into either six or nine troops, each led by four officers: captain, lieutenant, cornet and quartermaster. For combat, cavalry deployed in squadrons of 120–150 troopers. Massing as densely as possible, a squadron usually advanced on the enemy in two or three lines, although topography and circumstances might sometimes dictate a different deployment. At this time dragoons were mounted infantry, armed with swords and carbines. They employed horses for mobility but still generally dismounted for combat, although they sometimes fought on horseback.

In appearance the soldiers of the two armies would have looked very similar. The royal Stuart livery of red was the preferred uniform colour of both William's English and James's Irish regiments, but white, grey, yellow, green and blue uniforms were also all worn at the

A sabre

Trooper of Lord Galmoy's cavalry

Sarsfield's cavalry

Boyne. In an attempt to avoid confusion, the Williamites wore a sprig of green in their hats; the Jacobites wore a white paper symbolising their link with France. Soldiers were dressed in breeches, broad-brimmed hats, waistcoats and full-skirted coats. Infantrymen wore stockings and shoes. The mounted soldiers wore boots, and the cavalry sometimes protected their upper bodies with iron cuirasses, backplates and helmets.

Officers' uniforms were embellished with gold-washed buttons and braid on coats and hats. Infantry officers carried a spontoon, or half pike, as a symbol of authority. Regiments were distinguished by the distinctive 'facings' (the colour of the large, turned-back cuff of their uniform coats) and by the designs

Sergeant of Lord Dungan's Dragoons

Soldier of Lord Clare's Dragoons

Mounted grenadier

Cornet of Irish lifeguards

of their colours (rectangular infantry flags), standards (smaller rectangular cavalry flags) and guidons (dove-tailed dragoon flags). In the din of battle, basic orders were communicated by drums (infantry), trumpets (cavalry) and oboes (dragoons).

Both armies were reasonably well equipped for their task. William's field artillery, shipped in from Holland, comprised more than forty field-guns and a battery of howitzers. Artillery had the capability to fire various projectiles, but the most commonly used in a battlefield situation was a solid iron ball. Its weight, in pounds, determined a weapon's calibre. The Jacobites had at least sixteen field-guns, a dozen of which were French four-pounders, supplied for the campaign

Captain of Lord Bellew's regiment

with a complement of French gunners. The effective point-blank range (barrel parallel to the ground) of a cannon was 400 metres. Longer shots, up to 2,000 metres, were possible, but with reduced accuracy and velocity. Howitzers were innovative short-barrelled weapons, used for lobbing explosive shells.

The Jacobites had received a substantial supply of weapons and ammunition from France, although there were complaints about the poor condition of some of the muskets. The Williamites brought their own equipment, and great pains were taken to provide their army with adequate transport, commissariat and medical services. Between cavalry and transport, at least 10,000 horses would have accompanied William's army; the Jacobites must have had 5,000 horses or more. The fodder requirements meant neither field army could remain at any location for a protracted period.

War is an extension of politics. Thus a major objective of seventeenth-century warfare was to retain an army in being and at an adequate level of capability, thereby lending weight to political and diplomatic manoeuvring. The supply needs of the soldiers depended heavily – and in the case of their horses almost entirely – on local resources. Military campaigning was therefore concerned primarily with securing and conserving the territory – its own, or preferably its opponent's – the army needed for its subsistence. On the Continent this generally took the form of besieging or defending the sophisticated fortresses that had been constructed to guard this territory. Large-scale field battles were comparatively uncommon there, and usually related to fortress warfare.

Ensign of Gordon O'Neill's regiment

Feeding an army

Keeping an army supplied with adequate nourishment was the major challenge faced by seventeenth-century military planners, with daily food requirements equalling those of a sizeable city.

William provided each soldier with a daily one-pound bread ration. This was baked in the portable ovens of the Jewish army-catering contractor, Isaac Pereira of Amsterdam. Soldiers were expected to purchase their own food, and the cost of the bread was deducted from army pay. Other dietary needs were met from local resources, whether commandeered or purchased, and from the hoards of sutlers (provisions trader) accompanying the army.

On the Jacobite side, supply was part of the administrative responsibility of French *intendants*, who collected food in magazines. French military contractors were active, and limited amounts of food, brandy and wine were imported. Large quantities of livestock accompanied the army. The French brigade brought flour and bread ovens with the capacity to bake 8,000 rations daily.

In Ireland, however, the absence of modern fortresses forced the Jacobite army to defend its territory by fighting two major field battles: the Boyne and Aughrim. In such engagements the defending army was usually able to choose an advantageous battle site. In battle, an army was drawn up in two long lines, with infantry battalions in the centre and cavalry and dragoons on the wings, where their mobility could be used to outflank (*i.e.* extend beyond and around) the enemy, or to counter any such manoeuvre by their opponents. Field artillery softened up the opposing army before the infantry engaged, first with musket volleys and then at close quarters. Such combat was rarely conclusive – unless the cavalry succeeded in turning the enemy's flank. If this happened, the outflanked infantry would be forced to withdraw in good order, or risk destruction either through encirclement or, if its formation broke, from the sabres of the pursuing cavalry. This was the pattern at both the Boyne and Aughrim.

A field battle, once it commenced, was a bedlam of noise, violence and confusion. The clouds of gun smoke that enveloped the combatants obscured everyone's view, including that of the army commanders. Their ability to direct events was further hampered by communications that could proceed only at horse speed and were conveyed by word-of-mouth. As a consequence, subordinate generals, each entrusted with command of a section of the line, were expected to respond to challenges and opportunities as they occurred in

Infantry discharge a volley

their vicinity. Junior officers and ordinary soldiers had little overall concept of what was taking place. Their experience of battle was to obey orders, follow their leaders, stand their ground, discharge their weapons and then engage their immediate enemies hand-to-hand. Drums, trumpets and oboes were employed to convey routine commands above the din of battle. If a regiment became disordered, the soldiers were likely to panic and run, throwing away their arms and scattering 'like sheep flying before the wolf'.

A soldier's chances of losing his life from war, whether in battle or from disease (the biggest killer), was about one in five. Battle wounds came from sword cuts, penetration by firearms projectiles, pike and bayonet thrusts, broken limbs and burns from powder accidents. All regiments included a surgeon, and both armies had a hospital service. Amongst battle casualties, wounded survivors usually outnumbered fatalities. Psychiatric damage, which must have occurred, was an unknown concept and is unmentioned in the records of the time. Dead bodies were stripped and buried in

GRAND PRIOR'S — DRUMMER

Drummer of the Grand Prior's regiment

An engraving of the battle by Dirk Maas, an eyewitness

mass pits, unless quickly reclaimed by relatives or comrades. In all, war in the seventeenth century was a very different proposition from its equivalent today. The short range and low firepower of the weaponry of the period brought soldiers, when they engaged, into close physical contact with their opponents. Their immediate experience of battle was a *mêlée* of bodies, close fighting, smoke, noise, rearing horses, the screams of casualties and, most likely, sheer terror.

The battlefield

A river such as the Boyne, flowing from west to east, provided a convenient obstacle where the Jacobites could oppose the further advance south of the Williamite army. A river crossing, especially by infantry, depended on securing bridges and fords. At the Boyne most of the fighting took place in the vicinity of Oldbridge, but the two bridging points at Slane and Drogheda, 14km apart, defined the effective area of military operations, which also extended 5km south to the village of Duleek, where another bridge traversed the small River Nanny. Neither of the Boyne bridges was available to the Williamites: the bridge at Slane had been broken down, while at Drogheda a

An eighteenth-century view of the ford at Oldbridge

1,300-strong Jacobite garrison in the walled town blocked access to the bridge. However, at low tide the Boyne was fordable at several locations, notably at Oldbridge and across a string of islands stretching for more than 1km to its east, approximately to the point where a rivulet enters the Boyne below Drybridge. Another crossing point was at Rossnaree, 14km upstream from Oldbridge.

The high ground dominating the riverbanks provided both armies with good facilities for observation and gave the Williamites a handy artillery platform at Oldbridge. On the south bank, between Oldbridge and Rossnaree, a steep ridge close to the river presented a formidable obstacle to any Williamite crossing. At Oldbridge there was 'a very fine, fertile plain', which gave more space to deploy on the south bank, from where a long slope facilitated ascent to the high ground at Donore. At Drybridge, to the east, the ridge ran closer to the river again. Northwest of Rossnaree House there was also more open ground south of the river, although this may have been considerably less than now appears because quarrying in the early twentieth century further levelled the landscape.

One weakness in the Boyne as a defensive position was the great southern bend in the river between Rossnaree and the loop at Oldbridge, which allowed an aggressor, advancing south, to outflank a force defending the

Oldbridge fords and also threaten its line of withdrawal through Duleek. This drawback was considerably mitigated by a deep glen, formed from a rivulet that flowed northwards from Corballis into the Boyne at Roughgrange, and by Gillinstown Bog, possibly a more extensive wetland then than now, which lay west of Duleek. The glen and the bog were located roughly midway between Oldbridge and Slane and together they protected the Jacobite left flank to a depth of 2km.

Jacobite view of their position at the Boyne

'[King James camped with] his right towards Drogheda and his left up the river, and finding that post an indifferent good one (and indeed the country afforded no better), he set up his rest there and resolved to expect the enemy.'

King James II's memoirs

Although the principal topographical features remain much the same, there are significant differences between the modern landscape and that of the late seventeenth century. The construction of the Boyne navigation, partly channelled through a canal, has altered the appearance of the river and its banks. The islands immediately east of Oldbridge, then bare of vegetation, are now heavily overgrown. Drogheda, Slane and Duleek were far smaller and less sprawling urban centres than is the case today. Despite its name, there was no bridge at Oldbridge in 1690. A village of some houses which stood on the south bank of the river is now gone, although recent archaeological investigation has established its location. The seventeenth-century village of Donore was more than 1km north-east of the present village of that name. Its original site, south-east of Sheephouse, is marked by the ruined church and surrounding burial ground of old Donore.

There was extensive tillage in the river valley in the vicinity of Oldbridge, where there were large cornfields, and also at Rossnaree, alongside fallow fields. Bad roads and lack of drainage impeded movement, especially of wheeled vehicles, although troop deployment through the countryside was in general facilitated by a relative absence of field boundaries. Coupled with the paucity of trees, this further exposed the manoeuvres of both armies to the view of their opponents.

By the late seventeenth century the brutal treatment of the civilian population that had characterised earlier wars, while not entirely absent, was certainly much reduced. Nonetheless the presence of two armies, with their massive foraging and subsistence demands, was a disagreeable experience for the inhabitants of any locality. Houses large and small were vacated to accommodate senior officers. Meadows and crops were ravaged, food and livestock commandeered and occasional outrages perpetrated.

On the other hand, an army camp – with a population greater than most cities – was also a major commercial and social event. It attracted civilians of all sorts: wives and other women, children, sutlers and other traders, craftsmen, wagoners, civil and ecclesiastical dignitaries, every variety of riff-raff and those who were simply sociable or curious. The short range of weaponry and slowness of troop manoeuvres meant that civilian evacuation was strictly necessary only from the immediate combat zone. Spectators could observe a battle in comparative safety, and even play a role in its conduct. One account, for example, mentions the country people – presumably Williamite supporters on the north bank – calling out for horse to go to the support of the infantry that had crossed the river, a cry misheard by others as a halt order, which caused them to delay their advance for half-an-hour. While fighting continued, the Scots-Irish rabble from the Williamite camp moved amongst the dead and dying in search of plunder, which they sold in a nearby makeshift market.

It was prudent for civilians to withdraw if the army with which they were associated suffered a setback. In the wake of the battle of the Boyne, the English soldiers, in particular, raped women they came across and committed further atrocities against the peasants in their houses.

> **Williamite view of Jacobite position**
>
> 'Upon [King William] taking a view of the enemy, he observed that they were strongly posted and drawn up to great advantage; and saw plainly it would be a difficult matter to force them from their ground.'
>
> *Captain John Parker, Williamite officer*

The battle plans

The initiative at the Boyne lay with the Williamites. At their eve-of-battle council of war, William and his generals considered two alternative plans. The first, advocated by the duke of Schomberg, was to make an attack at Oldbridge in sufficient strength to draw the Jacobite army forward into the loop of the Boyne. Meanwhile, the bulk of the Williamite army, having moved four or five miles upstream under cover of darkness, would cross the river at, or near, Slane and attack the Jacobites in the flank and rear. The rival plan, put forward by Count Solms, was to make a frontal attack at Oldbridge with the whole army. Schomberg's plan was the most daring, and offered the possibility of annihilating the Jacobite army by trapping it between the Boyne and the sea.

William opted for a mixture of the two. A force of 7,000 men, largely cavalry, would be sent upstream at dawn under Count Meinhard Schomberg, but most of the army would be retained in the Oldbridge sector for the main attack. Both forces were to engage the enemy at about ten o'clock in the morning, a little after ebb tide. William had the decisions of the war council minuted and sent out to his generals during the night. Next day, events forced him to commit one third or more of his army on the right wing, so that in operation his initial plan was modified to resemble a classic pincers movement.

On the Jacobite side the French still favoured retreating beyond the River Shannon, but such a strategy remained politically difficult for James. The Boyne, in his view, offered 'an indifferent good' position, although he was concerned at the threat posed to his left flank by any Williamite move upstream. Inexplicably, the Jacobite high command was unaware of the protection to its flank afforded by the Gillinstown Bog/Roughgrange declivity. James's vacillation between the different views of his generals left Jacobite strategic planning unclear. The outcome of his eve-of-battle council of war was a decision to move the bulk of the army westwards the following morning, in the belief that the Williamite attack would be made upstream. The army's baggage was

---
Confusion over dates

Under the Julian calendar, still in use in Britain and Ireland in 1690, the battle of the Boyne was fought on 1 July 1690. By then, most of mainland Europe had adopted the modern Gregorian calendar. Prior to 1700 the discrepancy between the two calendars was ten days, so that under the modern calendar the battle was fought on 11 July, as indeed eye-witness reports of Continentals, using the new calendar, make clear. However, by the mid-eighteenth century, when the modern calendar was finally adopted in Britain and Ireland, the gap between the two had widened to eleven days. In the late 1790s the eleven-day, eighteenth-century discrepancy was incorrectly transposed to the seventeenth century, which accounts for the fact that the traditional commemoration date of the Boyne is now 12 July, rather than the preceding day, which is the actual anniversary. The fact that the other major military engagement of the war, the battle of Aughrim, was fought on 12 July 1691, according to the old calendar, has probably contributed to the confusion! The convention of modern historians, which is followed in this guide, is to date seventeenth-century events in Britain and Ireland according to the old calendar for the day and the month, while commencing the calendar year on 1 January, rather than 25 March, as used under the Julian calendar.

packed to facilitate this manoeuvre and not, as has been alleged, in anticipation of a hasty retreat to Dublin, although the possibility of withdrawal probably remained in the back of James's mind.

In the event, however, the right wing of the army was left to cover the Oldbridge crossings, but its artillery support was withdrawn. A sod breastwork was constructed at Oldbridge, but otherwise nothing was done to obstruct the crossings with, for example, partially submerged stakes, *chevaux-de-frises* and spiked caltrops, which would have crippled the cavalry. A better strategy might have been to post a strong Jacobite force at the Roughgrange declivity, or even in the vicinity of Slane/Rossnaree, to threaten the Williamite flank. Either disposition would have checked Meinhard Schomberg's advance, whilst leaving the bulk of the Jacobite army at Oldbridge to hold William at bay until the rising tide made many of the fords impassable to his infantry.

The councils of war agreed their decisions and retired. Come what may, the battle was set for the following morning, and one can only imagine that the troops passed a restless night, watching the flames on the opposite side of the river, hearing the impatient whinnying of the horses, the murmurs of talk among their rivals and wondering what the day of battle would bring.

PART 3:

The battle

If you are visiting the battlesite at Oldbridge, the suggested procedure is to tour the battlefield, following in numerical order the sequence of stands described below. Most stands have been selected to coincide with the location of Battle of the Boyne Project interpretative storyboards, which relate the course of events in their immediate vicinity and depict some of the action, personalities and different types of soldier involved.

Detail of a seventeenth-century military camp

Stand 1: Tullyallen Church

The stand is at the cemetery on the south side of the Roman Catholic Church of the Assumption at Tullyallen. This is accessed via a laneway opposite The Morning Star pub in the centre of the village.

The Jacobite position

Looking south from Tullyallen church, the high ground south of the Boyne is clearly visible. The ridge on the near side of the cement-works chimneys is Donore Hill. The 24,000-strong Jacobite army was camped along its lower contours, in two lines, parallel to the river. A force of such size, with tents, wagons, thousands of horses and other livestock and camp followers of all sorts, covered an immense area. When the battle started King James's headquarters were at Donore village, then situated at the eastern end of the hill's summit (approximately in line with the cement-works chimneys). On the morning of the battle most of the Jacobite army marched west, parallel to the river.

The Williamite camp

The Williamites camped along the ridge of high ground running through Tullyallen. An army of 36,000, camped in two lines, would have extended along 5km from the Drogheda–Dundalk road to the River Mattock. King William's personal accommodation was in an easily assembled 'itinerant house' of canvas and wood, which Sir Christopher Wren had designed specially for the campaign to afford the leader comfort and privacy, even on the battlefield.

Artillery bombardment

On the eve of the battle Williamite artillery was posted on a contour overlooking the Boyne, at the end of the sloping fields south of Tullyallen church. From about 5.00pm on the eve of the battle, the guns and howitzers bombarded the Jacobite positions across the river. Their range extended to part of the Jacobite camp. Gunfire was renewed the next day, when it was also directed at the Jacobite troops moving upstream. The Williamite artillery

Aerial view, looking north, with Tullyallen village near the top of the picture and fields sloping down from there to the Boyne at Oldbridge. King William's Glen is the tree-lined avenue at the centre. (Photo by Esler Crawford)

prevented significant contingents of Jacobite infantry from being posted on the open ground beside the river to meet an assault, and made life uncomfortable for a battalion posted in an advance position at Oldbridge village. Apart from this, the range was too long for the cannonade to have had much effect. The guns shown in the foreground of Dirk Maas's (see p. 28) contemporary engraving of the battle illustrate this phase of operations.

Commencement of the Williamite attack

At 6.00am on the day of the battle, Meinhard Schomberg's force departed in an early-morning mist from the western end of the Williamite camp towards Slane and Rossnaree. Initially he had about 7,000 men, but fears that his force would be overwhelmed later prompted William to reinforce it with a substantial body of infantry under General Douglas, leaving just two thirds of the Williamite army to mount the attack at Oldbridge. Later, at about 9.00am, as the day was growing sunny and eventually 'excessive hot', the main party of Williamite infantry, their drums beating, advanced in columns from their camp down the slopes from Tullyallen to the river crossings below. The Dutch footguards appear to have advanced through King William's Glen, a declivity that is the route of the modern road. In 1690 it was linked to Tullyallen by a lane, now much over-grown, running from south-west of the church.

Stand 2: Oldbridge ford (north bank)

Return to the village and turn left at The Morning Star pub. Proceed for 0.5km to the next crossroads at the end of the village, and turn left to descend for 1.5km through King William's Glen to the iron road bridge that crosses the Boyne. The stand is on a commanding bluff on the north bank, overlooking the river. Access is through a wooden gate on the left of the short road approaching the bridge.

King William wounded

Looking north from this viewing point at Oldbridge, the tall trees behind the estate wall at the south-west end of King William's Glen mask a mound of high ground. It was here on the eve of the battle, while on reconnaissance in the early afternoon, that William was grazed on his right shoulder by a Jacobite cannon ball, fired from one of two guns deployed near the south river bank. Most accounts refer to the ball as a 6-pounder, although it is more likely that it was fired from one of the French 4-pounders. The shot drew blood and naturally caused much commotion in the group accompanying the king. William himself remarked drily (in Dutch) that it was as well the shot had come no closer. After the wound was dressed he resumed his reconnaissance. The incident had taken more out of him than was generally admitted, however. On returning to his tent he was so weak and fatigued he had to be lifted from his horse to rest, although he later remounted and rode through the camp to show his men that he had survived the incident. On the other side of the river the Irish observed the commotion immediately after the king was hit, and gave a great shout (their usual pre-battle practice); William's death was celebrated prematurely in Paris when news of the incident arrived there.

King William III's near escape

'Posterity may have difficulty in believing how this great prince escaped with his life. It must be mentioned that the enemy having perceived through their field glasses that the king was reconnoitring their camp, and advancing towards the bank of the river in order to reconnoître the fords, pointed their artillery at the group. The second shot, which they fired, almost overthrew the king. The ball passed so near his back that his doublet, his waistcoat and his coat were burnt about a hand's breadth, and the skin grazed so closely that it bled. Those about his majesty thought he was dangerously wounded, but he said with great coolness: 'It is nothing, but the ball came very near.' The king then asked for his cloak, in order to hide the hole burnt in his coat, and went on further. After having received his wound he went on two or three hours longer on horseback, lest the report that he was wounded should spread through the camp and alarm the troops. Having reached the extremity of the trenches he retired into his tent. The doctors wished to bleed him. He laughed at them and called for his own surgeon, who applied a plaster to the wound.'

Jean Payen de la Fouleresse,
Danish diplomat

The assault across the river

The main Williamite assault across the Boyne was on a 2km front, running from east of the viewing point as far as Drybridge, about 500m east of the motorway road bridge. The attack was spearheaded by the three battalions of William's Dutch footguards, under Count Solms, which approached the riverbank under the cover of King William's Glen. At about 10.00am, marching eight or ten abreast, they entered the water, at Oldbridge ford, approximately 300m east of the present bridge. They were followed down-

The Dutch guards ford the Boyne at Oldbridge (Illustration by Richard Hook)

stream, at staggered intervals, by successive brigades of infantry: two Huguenot regiments and Colonel Thomas St John's Londonderry foot, which crossed via Grove Island; Sir John Hanmer's English foot and the count of Nassau's Dutch, which crossed via Yellow Island; and the Danish infantry, which crossed in the vicinity of the new suspension bridge. The crossings took place somewhat after low tide. The Dutch were waist-deep at the ford, whereas the Danes, entering the Boyne somewhat later and to the east, found the riverbed boggy and were soon in water up to their armpits. Their commander, the duke of Würtemburg, kept dry by crossing the river on the shoulders of two grenadiers. The Williamite second line followed the front line across the river.

While in the water, the Williamites encountered comparatively little resistance from the Jacobites, deployed, as they were, well back from the river out of artillery range. The infantry regiment posted at Oldbridge village fired a single musket volley at the lead battalion of Dutch footguards in the river, inflicting a few casualties. At about noon William himself

crossed at Drybridge, east of the new suspension bridge, by swimming across the river with the 2,000 cavalry and dragoons of his left wing.

Stand 3: Oldbridge village

Proceed across the iron bridge to Oldbridge House, from where a walkway leads to the site of Oldbridge village beside the modern entrance gate.

Oldbridge village and the cornfield

Prior to the battle the Jacobite army camped on the slopes south of Oldbridge. The high command feared a Williamite flanking movement to the west, which would threaten James II's army with encirclement in the bend of the Boyne. It was decided to move the army westwards to prevent this possibility. On the morning of the battle the dawn movement upstream of Meinhard

Aerial view of the ford and site of village at Oldbridge, looking east. (Photo by Esler Crawford)

Schomberg's force injected this manoeuvre with new urgency. At 8.00am the left wing of the army, including the French brigade and one third of the artillery, commenced its march upstream, followed somewhat later by the army centre, accompanied by King James.

This left only the right wing of the army – one third of its strength – to defend the Oldbridge sector against two thirds of the larger Williamite army. Tyrconnell, commander of the Jacobite right wing, had four regiments of cavalry, two of dragoons and about seven infantry battalions, perhaps 7,000–8,000 men in all. Most of the troops were drawn up on a plateau behind the ridge of high ground, about 1km south of the river. They were without artillery support because James had ordered the ten French guns remaining at Oldbridge to be withdrawn, much to the surprise of Laisné, the artillery commander. James's intention was to preserve the guns from capture, but this was in the context of a mistaken belief that the main battle would be fought upstream, and that the Jacobite right wing would shortly follow the rest of the army in that direction.

The initial fighting in this sector was in the vicinity of the small village of Oldbridge, beside the ford of the same name. (The village was removed from the landscape in the course of eighteenth-century estate improvement. Archaeological excavation has pinpointed its position however, and skeletal frames mark some of the house sites.) The village's houses and gardens provided cover from the Williamite artillery for the earl of Clanricard's infantry, one of the few Jacobite units deployed in a forward position near the river. A breastwork of sods had been erected across the road leading up from the ford. The defenders at Oldbridge fired off a volley at the lead battalion of Dutch footguards as it crossed the river, but the Dutch pressed on, undeterred, and the Jacobites withdrew through the village to a cornfield that lay between the village and the plateau. There they exchanged further fire with the advancing Dutch before again withdrawing. The Dutch took up a defensive formation in the cornfield.

The withdrawal of the Jacobite artillery

'One of the things which also contributed to making this [Oldbridge] crossing easier to force is that the king, at the commencement of his march to the left, sent an order to M. Laisné to withdraw the artillery from the batteries, where I had posted it. This surprised him so much that he sought confirmation. Having received it, he obeyed the order, but the delay prevented him from following our troops [to the left], and he was compelled to withdraw by the main road to Dublin, which he did in a very orderly fashion.'

Marquis de La Hoguette,
French lieutenant general

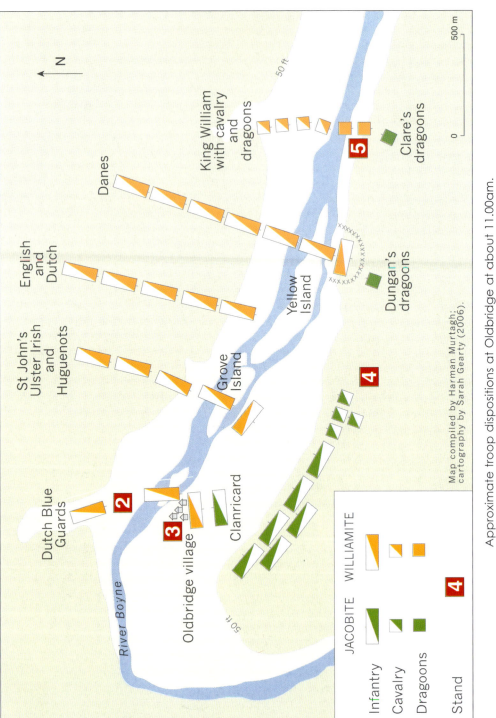

Approximate troop dispositions at Oldbridge at about 11.00am.

Map compiled by Harman Murtagh; cartography by Sarah Gearty (2006).

Map labels

N

St John's Ulster Irish and Huguenots

English and Dutch

Danes

King William with cavalry and dragoons

Dutch Blue Guards

Grove Island

Yellow Island

Clare's dragoons

Dungan's dragoons

River Boyne

Oldbridge village

Clanricard

50 ft

50 ft

500 m

0

2

3

4

5

Legend

JACOBITE WILLIAMITE

Infantry

Cavalry

Dragoons

Stand 4

Stand 4: Groggin's Field

From Oldbridge village ascend the ridge to the south, where most of the Jacobite right wing was stationed on the plateau behind. From this ridge walk east across the Oldbridge–Sheephouse road to the Groggin's Field, from where there is a fine prospect of the combat area on the south side of the river.

Infantry counter-attack

As the Williamite infantry took up position in the cornfield south of Oldbridge it was counter-attacked by the Jacobite infantry, which descended from the plateau 'with a great shout', but was 'much galled ... and several times put into disorder' by the Williamite artillery, as it advanced. The Irish footguards closed with their Dutch counterparts; musket volleys were exchanged at close range; and there was some hand-to-hand fighting in which several Jacobite officers were casualties. The rest of the Jacobite infantry performed badly. Boisseleau's Cork regiment was reluctant to advance. Richard Hamilton, second-in-command of the right wing, was unable to inspire his men to enter the river against the Huguenots. Further downstream, Lord Antrim's regiment failed to attack Hanmer's and Nassau's

The Dutch footguards on the south bank

'The king had not passed the river, but was looking upon the action and in great concern for his blue guards, who had marched to the left between the two houses and the river and were forming as fast as they could to receive a body of Irish horse that was coming towards them upon a full trot. The king was in a good deal of apprehension for them, there not being a hedge or ditch before them, nor any of our horse to support them, and I was so near his majesty to hear him say softly to himself: 'my poor guards, my poor guards, my poor guards', as the enemy were coming down upon them, but when he saw them stand their ground and fire upon them by platoons, so that the horse were forced to run away, he breathed out as people are used to do after holding their breath upon a fright or suspense, and said he had seen his guards do what he had never seen foot do in his life.'

George Clarke,
secretary at war to William III

infantry. The infantry action appears to have lasted about an hour. Eventually, the Jacobites gave away and fell back to the plateau through the gunsmoke. D'Hocquincourt, their French brigadier, was killed and the battalions that had been engaged played no further part in the battle.

Aerial view, looking west, of sites of Williamite infantry crossings at Oldbridge. The tree-covered areas are islands. (Photo by Esler Crawford)

Dragoon withdrawal

Two regiments of Jacobite dragoons, Dungan's and Clare's, were deployed on the right wing. Neither did well. A volley from the Danes cleared Dungan's men from the riverbank. A cannon shot killed Lord Dungan as he withdrew, after which his demoralised regiment was reluctant, for a time, to re-engage the enemy. Soon afterwards, on the extreme right, Lord Clare's regiment 'that seemed the loveliest in the world' made only a feeble defence against the Williamite cavalry at Drybridge, before riding off 'without a backward glance'. Later, three units probably formed part of the force that repulsed the Williamite attack on Donore.

Cavalry counter-attack

It was left to the four cavalry regiments of the Jacobite right wing to mount the main resistance. They cannot have numbered more than 1,200 sabres, but a ration of brandy stiffened the troopers' resolve. Tyrconnell, a portly sixty-year-old, bravely led his three-squadron regiment against the Dutch. Lord Dover's troop of horseguards, amounting to a further squadron, may have accompanied him. From the north bank of the river, King William watched apprehensively as the armies engaged. The cavalry advanced at full trot, but failed to break through the disciplined Dutch, who fired several volleys in ranks and by platoon before fixing bayonets to fend off the attack. A Williamite observer wrote: 'Tyrconnell's regiment behaved themselves well, but our Dutch [were] like angels.' The Dutch must have suffered from the pistols of the cavaliers, which were fired at close range, as there were considerable casualties on both sides.

Nearby, a squadron or more of Parker's regiment – a Jacobite unit whose officers were mainly English – engaged the Huguenots. The French Protestants were without pikes, bayonets, or *chevaux-de-frise* and probably lacked the discipline of the Dutch. Once their muskets

The Jacobite cavalry

'The horse did their duty with great bravery, and though they did not break the enemy's foot, it was more by reason of the ground not being favourable, than for want of vigour, for after they had been repulsed by the foot, they rallied again, and charged the enemy's horse and beat them every charge: Tyrconnell's and Parker's troops suffered the most on this occasion. Sutherland's regiment (though wounded himself) suffered not much, having to do only with the enemy's horse, which he soon repulsed; in fine they were so roughly handled and overpowered by numbers, that at last they were quite broke.'

King James II's memoirs

The conflict at Oldbridge at 11.00am, viewed from Groggin's Field: the Williamite infantry ford the River Boyne and take up position on the south bank; the Jacobite infantry withdraws. The Jacobite cavalry attacks the Williamites. (Illustration by Richard Hook)

were discharged, they were vulnerable to the Irish cavalry. Seeing this, the riders broke through their lines and inflicted heavy casualties. The most prominent was Colonel La Caillemotte, who was mortally wounded. One Jacobite squadron penetrated as far as Oldbridge village, but was 'mostly cut to pieces' in a withering musket fire as it sought to retire. St John's Londonderry regiment was also attacked, and Berwick led his squadron of horseguards against Hanmer's regiment as it sought to establish itself on the south bank opposite Yellow Island. A further force of sixty troopers drove back a squadron of Danish cavalry that had crossed the river in advance of its infantry. The latter withstood a cavalry charge, secure behind a barrier of *chevaux-de-frise* it had carried across the river in sections and assembled hastily upon coming ashore.

The Jacobite cavalry action at Oldbridge lasted almost an hour and stalled the Williamite infantry attack on the south bank of the Boyne. The cavalry put in three or four charges in all and suffered heavy casualties. Sheldon, the cavalry commander, had two horses killed under him. They were preparing to

mount yet another attack, when the threat to their flank from William's crossing of the Boyne at Drybridge forced them to break off the action at Oldbridge and withdraw uphill to Donore.

The death of Schomberg

Marshal Schomberg, the senior Williamite general, and a small staff crossed the Boyne at Oldbridge, apparently in advance of the Huguenots, whom he urged across the river with the words, '*Allons, mes amis, rappelez votre courage et vos ressentiments, voilà vos persécuteurs*' ('Onwards comrades, recall your courage and your resentments, there are your persecutors!'). Wearing his blue Garter ribbon, the old marshal made a prominent target. He received two sabre cuts to the head before a bullet in the neck killed him instantly. Williamite accounts suggest he was the victim of a stray shot from his own side; the Jacobites credited his death to Sir Charles O'Toole of their horseguards. A stone near the gate of Oldbridge House, bearing the date 1690, traditionally marks the site of his death, although the actual location may have been some distance to the east.

Another victim was Rev. George Walker, who had been closely involved in Derry's defence in 1689. Crossing the Boyne about the same time as

The death of Schomberg

Schomberg, he died from a shot in the stomach.

Schomberg's body was rescued by an *aide-de-camp*, whereas Walker's was immediately stripped by the Scots-Irish rabble that followed the army. William showed no emotion on being informed of Schomberg's death beyond indicating that he did not want word of the event to spread. After the battle, however, he sympathised with Meinhard Schomberg and was reported to have wept and declared that he, too, had lost a father. Walker, who was designate bishop of Derry, William dismissed as a fool who had no business on a battle-field. Schomberg was buried in St Patrick's Cathedral, Dublin, where his

Rev. George Walker

monument can still be seen. It was erected at the expense of the cathedral chapter. The fulsome Latin inscription, penned by Dean Swift, includes the information that requests to his family to contribute to the cost were ignored.

Stand 5: Drybridge

From Oldbridge House proceed to the road running along the north bank of the Boyne canal and river. Head east and pass beneath the new motorway bridge. The stand is 0.3km further on, at the point where the road turns inland away from the river.

William leads 2,000 cavalry across the Boyne

The stand overlooks the point where William III crossed the Boyne. The beleaguered Williamite infantry, which had forded the Boyne in the vicinity of Oldbridge, had been calling for cavalry support. At noon, William responded by personally leading the cavalry and dragoons of his left wing across the river, about 2km downstream. The location is generally called Drybridge, a name that comes from a crossing-point on a nearby rivulet. William's force comprised Dutch, Danish, Huguenot and Enniskillen cavalry, and at least two regiments of dragoons, perhaps 2,000 horsemen in all.

The topography of the river and its banks at Drybridge remains largely unchanged, and shows that the passage would not have been easy. It took place in a rising tide, forcing most of the horses to swim. William himself

King William III crosses the Boyne

'When this great and valiant prince came to the river side at the head of four troops of Enniskillen horse, one regiment of Danish horse and another of English foot, he drew his sword and spoke thus to the Enniskilleners: 'I have heard a great deal of your bravery, and now I make no doubt I shall be an eyewitness of it.' The four captains thereupon requested him not to expose his person to so great a danger by crossing the river within shot of the enemy. 'No', said he, 'I will see you over the river'.

When the king was in the middle of the river a regiment of Irish dragoons, which were posted upon a rising ground within shot of the ford, fired at him, and immediately retreated to a body of horse drawn up at a little distance behind them in a fallow field. A bullet hit the cap of the king's pistol. Captain Blachford had his horse killed under him and there was no man killed, which was all the execution done here as far as I could learn.

As soon as the king came up to the place, which the Irish dragoons had quitted, he drew up the four troops of the Enniskillen horse, and then ordered them to attack the aforesaid body of Irish horse. Immediately they marched up to the enemy with great intrepidity, and charged them sword in hand; upon which the Irish gave away, and retreated in great disorder.'

Rev. John Richardson,
Williamite eye-witness

Aerial view of Drybridge, looking east. King William crossed with his cavalry close to the small island near the top of the picture. (Photo by Esler Crawford)

got into difficulties on the south bank, and had to be rescued after his mount became stuck in the soft mud. He was asthmatic, and the incident left him noticeably out of breath. Despite the stiffness of his shoulder wound, he drew his sword to lead the advance.

The high ground immediately south of the Boyne at Drybridge would have benefited a determined defence of the crossing, but Lord Clare's dragoons withdrew after firing a single volley. William then led the cavalry uphill to threaten the Jacobite right flank. This was the decisive move in this sector of the battle, as it forced the Jacobites to break off their counter-attack at Oldbridge and retire to the high ground at Donore. The Williamite infantry, which had been contained for two hours on the south side of the river, was now free to advance.

Stand 6: old Donore Church and burial ground

Proceed west back along the road towards Oldbridge, turning south after 1.3km at the first turn to the left, in the direction of Donore village. After 2km, turn left at a T-junction. After 0.3km, at a sharp right-hand turn, there is a cottage on the left with an iron gate. Proceed through the gate and down a narrow lane to old Donore church and burial ground, a walk of 1km. The stand is at the south-east corner of the burial ground, overlooking the new motorway bridge.

Confusion at Donore

Old Donore church and burial ground marks the approximate site of Donore village in 1690. It was here that James II took up his position before the battle started. However, he moved off to the west with the centre of his army shortly before the Williamite assault on Oldbridge commenced. The prospect towards the modern suspension bridge offers a good view of the sloping ground up which William III led his cavalry after successfully crossing the Boyne at Drybridge. His advance threatened to envelop the Jacobite cavalry if it remained committed to battle at Oldbridge. To defend their flank, the Jacobites were obliged to withdraw to the commanding ground at Donore. In a sense the cavalry action here was part of the resistance by the Jacobite right wing. In reality, it amounted to a fighting retreat that bought time for the Jacobite infantry to retire from the Oldbridge sector to Duleek.

Aerial view looking northeast from old Donore. King William led his cavalry up the slope just east of the suspension bridge against Donore village, then located near the walled churchyard at the bottom of the picture. (Photo by Esler Crawford)

Incident at Donore

'His majesty was here in the crowd of all, drawing his sword and animating those that fled to follow him. His danger was great amongst the enemy's guns, which killed thirty of the Enniskilleners on the spot. Nay one of the Enniskilleners came with a pistol cocked to his majesty, till he called out: 'what, are you angry with your friends?'

Sir Robert Southwell,
secretary of state for Ireland

It is not possible, except in a general way, to relate the action to the modern landscape. Undoubtedly Donore was the scene of a very sharp, if confused, fight. Old walls, holes in the ground and dungpits, all now gone, impeded the Williamites. Their initial advance was checked by a Jacobite cavalry charge, probably delivered by Sutherland's regiment, which had not been committed at Oldbridge. William then placed himself at the head of the Enniskillen cavalry. They were enthusiastic but inexperienced, and when he wheeled off to bring up the Dutch cavalry, the Enniskilleners followed him instead of completing their attack. Their move threw the Dutch into disorder. Subsequently, the Enniskilleners and the Danes mistook each other for the enemy and became involved in a *mêlée*. At one point William came close to being shot by an Enniskillen trooper.

A party of Dutch cavalry, which Lieutenant General Ginkel led along a lane to the east of Donore, was driven back by the Jacobites, who 'came up very boldly' until halted by a volley from the Williamite dragoons. The Huguenot cavalry was repulsed from a Jacobite strongpoint, enclosed by a ditch and bank and lined with dragoons. Presumably drawn from the regiments of Dungan and Clare, although it is also possible that a third unnamed dragoon regiment on the Jacobite right wing was involved. The engagement at Donore lasted half-an-hour. The Jacobites then withdrew, probably through Platin, to gain the road linking Drogheda with Duleek. William's cavalry followed in close pursuit.

Further engagement at Platin

The final engagement of the Jacobite right wing was at Platin Castle, now marked by the cement factory, more than 1km south of Donore. It was probably here that General Richard Hamilton, placing himself at the head of the remnants of the Jacobite cavalry, fought a rearguard action. Heavily outnumbered, his counter-attack failed. He was wounded and made prisoner within sight of William, who treated him graciously. It seems to have been in

Jacobite dragoons resist Huguenot cavalry at Donore
(Illustration by Richard Hook)

the same skirmish that the duke of Berwick had his horse killed under him and 'was beat down in the midst of the enemy, where he was trampled upon and bruised, and was with great difficulty saved by the assistance of a trooper', who brought him to safety. After this, the Jacobite cavalry and dragoons followed the infantry of the right wing towards Duleek.

William may have decided to wait for his infantry to come up from Oldbridge. Certainly, he did not press home the pursuit immediately, and only recommenced the attack after he had rendezvoused north of Duleek with the cavalry from the right wing.

Consideration of events in the Oldbridge–Donore sector

The Jacobite high command had underestimated the strength of the force retained by William for the assault on Oldbridge. The transfer of forces to the left wing and the withdrawal of artillery fatally weakened their capability to resist the strong Williamite attack. Little was done to fortify the riverbank, while inadequate reconnaissance seems to have blinded them to the possibility of a significant Williamite crossing at Drybridge. Except at Oldbridge, where the village offered some limited cover, the Williamite artillery ensured that the Jacobite infantry had to be held well back from the Boyne. This meant the Williamite infantry battalions encountered very little resistance as they crossed the fordable river and established themselves on the south bank.

Once there, however, they were contained: first by the remaining Jacobite infantry, then by the cavalry, until William's crossing at Drybridge threatened the Jacobite flank. William had sent the larger part of his cavalry upstream with Meinhard Schomberg. The depleted force he committed at Donore and Platin overcame, but was too weak to overrun, a spirited Jacobite defence. The Jacobite right wing thus evaded entrapment in the Boyne bend and made good its escape.

Stand 7: Rossnaree

The next stand is at Rossnaree, 10km west of old Donore. From old Donore church proceed to the next T-junction and turn right for the modern village of Donore. Turn right at St Mary's Roman Catholic church. The route will take you through the village and then parallel to the Boyne, past Brú na Bóinne Interpretive Centre. Notice the sharp ridge of high ground on your left, which would have made it very difficult for troops that crossed the river to deploy on the south bank. Keep right at the two road junctions in the vicinity of Rossnaree

House, and watch out for a storyboard on your right, 1.5km from the second junction. From this stand Slane bridge is clearly in view to the west, and the mound of the megalithic tomb of Knowth is visible across the river to the north-east. On the right, south of the river and opposite Knowth, an area of lowland can be seen, which provided space for cavalry to deploy.

Meinhard Schomberg crosses the Boyne at Rossnaree

A more aggressive Jacobite defence might have included occupation of the high ground at Slane by a strong left wing. Instead, the Jacobites confined themselves to breaking down the bridge there, and covered their left flank with the single dragoon regiment of Sir Neil O'Neill – less than 600 men – which was posted in isolation on the south side of the river at Rossnaree. At dawn on the morning of the battle, Meinhard Schomberg led a force of 7,000 or more, predominantly cavalry and dragoons, westwards along the uplands north of the river to the ford of Rossnaree, which he reached at about 8.00am. Up to this point the uplands immediately south of the river had prevented him from attempting a crossing. South-west of Knowth, however, in the river bend beside the modern Rossnaree House, Schomberg saw the 'very fine plain' he needed for the deployment of his forces on the south bank. Although heavily outnumbered, O'Neill's dragoons offered a spirited resistance. Initially they fought on foot, firing several volleys at

Sir Neil O'Neill

the Williamite mounted grenadiers and dragoons in the river. Later they mounted up, possibly for the final phase of their resistance and certainly for their withdrawal. Their resistance lasted nearly an hour, and they retired only when the Williamites brought their accompanying field guns into play. A ball shattered O'Neill's thigh, a serious wound that proved fatal.

Back at Oldbridge, when word arrived that Meinhard Schomberg was already across the river, William sent orders that he should press ahead with his advance. In order to allay anxiety that he might be overwhelmed by the Jacobites, whose forces could be seen moving west in large numbers, General Douglas was sent to reinforce him with a sizeable contingent of infantry. Accounts of the numbers involved vary, but it seems that about one third of the

Aerial view of the Boyne between Oldbridge and Rosnaree, looking southwest. The ridge of high ground extending to the right from the farmyard at the centre of the picture prevented Meinhard Schomberg crossing the river. The wooded area on the left of the picture shows the declivity at Roughgrange that later prevented the armies from engaging. (Photo by Esler Crawford)

Williamite army was eventually deployed on the right wing. News that a large body of Williamites had forced the crossing at Rossnaree convinced James II that he was threatened with envelopment. He therefore ordered his centre to follow the left wing of his army upstream, and himself brought up the rear with the reserve. Two thirds of the Jacobite army, including the French brigade, was now committed to shoring up the left flank. Meanwhile, Meinhard Schomberg cautiously advanced south-eastwards, in the direction of the Jacobite forces.

Stand 8: Roughgrange

Proceed east, back along the road towards Brú na Bóinne, for 4km until you come to Roughgrange Farm on the right-hand side of the road, where the end of a wide ravine is visible immediately east of the farmhouse.

Stand-off between the two armies

Better reconnaissance by the Jacobites would have shown James that his left wing was naturally protected by a deep ravine at Roughgrange, stretching south from the Boyne for 2km and with a further fork to the south-west. Both forces drew up in two lines on either side of the ravine, at right-angles to the main river. Although the Jacobite soldiers, French and Irish, were calling out to go into combat, a stand-off ensued, until James II was informed of Tyrconnell's difficulties at Oldbridge. He then ordered an immediate attack, only to be told by Sarsfield that the ravine was impassable. This was a crucial turn in events, as it prevented the Jacobite army engaging its opponents where it enjoyed local numerical superiority.

In the early afternoon, with the arrival of Douglas's infantry to reinforce Meinhard Schomberg, the Williamite right wing began to move south again, threatening to outflank the Jacobites. Progress was slow: the Williamite cavalry was obstructed by 'great ditches' enclosing cornfields, while the infantry blundered into the 'damned deep bog' at Gillinstown, from which it emerged only with some difficulty. Had Meinhard Schomberg conducted a reconnaissance while he awaited Douglas, the obstructions ahead would have been revealed and he might have chosen instead to advance along the Slane–Dublin road, which would have been speedier and more effective. In response, the whole Jacobite left wing, now also comprising the forces from

Aerial view of the Boyne near Rossnaree, looking southwest. The fields enclosed by the bend in the Boyne provided the plain that Meinhard Schomberg needed to deploy his troops on the south bank. The tumulus of Knowth is at the bottom right-hand corner of the picture. (Photo by Esler Crawford)

the army's centre, withdrew parallel to the advancing Williamites. It marched in two columns to Duleek and James, who must have ordered this move, rode with it, accompanied by Lauzun.

Stand 9: Duleek Bridge

Proceed east from Roughgrange Farm, turning right almost immediately at the next junction. From there, follow the narrow road south for 4.5km to Duleek. Turn left into the village and then right at the east end, where the road signed 'Ashbourne' leads to St Mary Magdalen Bridge, over the River, Nanny. The stand is north of the river, at the bridge.

Jacobite withdrawal across the River Nanny

In 1690 the Nanny at Duleek was 'a deep straight rivulet, very soft in the bottom, and [with] high banks on each side'. It has since been drained and is quite unimpressive, but at the time of the battle it seems to have presented a formidable obstacle, passable only via the narrow, meandering bridge dating from 1587, which is still extant although somewhat altered. James II's party was first across; at Lauzun's urging, the king pressed ahead with a cavalry escort to make good his escape to Dublin.

Behind, the remaining cavalry sought to protect the rear of the infantry column from harrassment by the Williamite cavalry and dragoons. The withdrawal across the bridge must have been a nail-bitingly slow operation. It was effected in an orderly fashion, however, until the fleeing cavalry

The French brigade at Duleek

'We posted our seven battalions as they emerged from the river crossing, each according to the ground that suited them, to counter an attack by the enemy. I ordered Zurlauben's regiment that was the last to come across to leave their grenadiers in the hedges behind them to discourage over-eager pursuit. The cavalry behind us, observing our deployment, formed up for battle, some on our flanks and some to our rear. We also placed our five cannon between two of our battalions to open fire on the enemy once they were posted... We held our ground until the crossing was completely clear and the entire Irish infantry... had passed and was far ahead of us on the road... to Dublin... There was nothing else to do [then] but to withdraw in an orderly fashion.'

Marquis de La Hoguette,
French lieutenant general

The roads converge on St Mary Magdalen bridge at Duleek, in the foreground. The river was considerably wider in 1690. (Photo by Esler Crawford)

The French brigade and available artillery check the Williamite pursuit at Duleek (Illustration by Richard Hook)

of the Jacobite right wing, led by Berwick, 'came on so unexpected and with such speed, some firing their pistols' that the rearmost portion of the retreating left wing was thrown into confusion. A dozen infantry regiments broke up in disarray and took to their heels, casting aside their weapons and equipment to speed their getaway. The subsequent recovery of 4,000–5,000 discarded pikes and muskets is indicative that about one quarter of the Jacobite infantry was involved in the collapse. But contrary to what is often stated, much of the army withdrew in good order; disintegration set in only during the days that followed, as it retreated towards Limerick.

The French brigade covers the retreat

The Jacobite retreat was covered by the French brigade, which was directed by Lieutenant General de La Hoguette. At Duleek, flanked by Jacobite cavalry, the seven French infantry battalions took up position on the ridge immediately south of the bridge. The five remaining artillery pieces of the Jacobite left wing – the

sixth had become bogged down and was abandoned – were posted between two of the battalions. Their fire checked the advance of the pursuing Williamites as they crossed the bridge. Preceded by the guns, the French then retired south in good order. When the Williamite cavalry pressed close, the French turned again, probably at Naul, and once more halted the pursuit, this time with a musket volley. The disciplined, fighting withdrawal of the French enabled their Irish allies to make good their escape. It was the only significant contribution the French brigade made to the battle, or indeed to the entire campaign in Ireland.

William at Duleek

King William took part in the final pursuit and had yet another 'near-miss' at Naul, when a bullet shot off the heel of his boot. Halted there by the French and with dusk closing in, he called off the pursuit and returned to Duleek. He was cheerful, only showing emotion when given an account of Marshal Schomberg's death. It was too late to bring forward the army's baggage, including William's portable house. Surrounded by his Dutch footguards, the king spent the night in the carriage of his dull brother-in-law, prince George of Denmark. The Williamite soldiers bivouacked in the open, grouped around fires fuelled with discarded Jacobite weapons. The walled town of Drogheda surrendered the next day on terms that required its garrison to disarm but allowed it to retire to the Jacobite stronghold of Athlone in County Westmeath.

PART 4:

Significance and aftermath

King William's victory

William III undoubtedly won the battle of the Boyne. His enemies were in retreat, leaving him master of the field. Soon afterwards Dublin, the rest of Leinster and east Munster also came under his control. However, his pincers movement on the battlefield – which may have evolved as events unfolded rather than been thoroughly planned – missed the opportunity to trap the Jacobite army north of the River Nanny. Some Williamite sources offered the unconvincing explanation that William wished to avoid the embarrassment of capturing his father-in-law. Considering the large number of soldiers involved at the Boyne, casualties were light: perhaps 1,500 killed or badly wounded, of which two thirds were Jacobites. There were a number of prominent casualties on both sides, while the Williamites also took some prisoners. The Jacobites saved their artillery and regimental colours, but lost their baggage and large numbers of discarded weapons.

William was a brave and even charismatic leader, but his failure to annihilate the Jacobite army at the Boyne showed him to have been an indifferent general. He failed to define the precise role of Meinhard Schomberg before sending him west, where he was out of sight and hard to contact or reinforce. At Oldbridge, earlier cavalry support by William for his exposed infantry on the south bank would have given the Jacobites less time to make good their retreat. Against that, however, it could be argued that if the Jacobite cavalry had suffered less attrition, William's horsemen would have been in danger of being overwhelmed on their ascent from Drybridge to Donore. But this, at least in part, was due to the fact that William had committed so much of his cavalry strength to Meinhard Schomberg on the distant right wing. Furthermore, his tactical handling of the situation at Donore was muddled and inept, and by his failure to engage in close pursuit he allowed the Jacobite right wing to make good its escape.

William arriving in Dublin

Nonetheless, the enemy was routed. Flushed with victory, William seems to have overestimated his success. A week after the Boyne, in an ill-judged declaration made from his camp at Finglas, he offered the Jacobite officers only unconditional surrender. This was unacceptable while their army remained intact, whereas a more generous peace offer might have secured a positive response. William's intransigence probably prolonged the war in Ireland for another year: an advantage to Louis XIV which he secured at very little extra cost.

The Boyne was hailed as an important victory for the Grand Alliance. Contrary to what is often said, it was not celebrated by the singing of *Te Deums* in Rome, but only in the Austrian cathedrals of William's ally, the emperor. This triumphalism did not meet with the approval of the new pope, Alexander VIII, who was anxious for reconciliation with Louis XIV.

King James's defeat

If William had made clumsy mistakes, James II's tactical handling of the Jacobite army was infinitely worse. Amongst the obvious shortcomings were:

taking the field with an army that was too small; poor reconnaissance; belated and then excessive response to the threat to the left wing; failure to fortify the crossings; deployment of inadequate forces at Oldbridge; premature withdrawal of most of the artillery; absence of a proper battle plan; and uncertainty as to whether or not to give battle at all. All that can be said is that the army was preserved, while bolder or more imaginative handling might have led to its entrapment and destruction.

Allegations of physical cowardice on the part of James are misplaced. He did not desert his army at the Boyne, but remained with it, at least as far as Duleek. James's subsequent hasty departure from Ireland – his sole remaining kingdom – dramatised William's victory and further diminished his own prestige. However, his flight was politically motivated: with all possibility of a restoration through Ireland at an end, the only way James could recover his English throne was via France and on board a French fleet. Nevertheless, he was undoubtedly demoralised by his Boyne experience. His speech before he left Dublin was ungracious and discouraging. He accused the Irish of not standing by him, and advised them to settle with William on whatever terms they could obtain.

The defeat at the Boyne disillusioned Irish Catholics with James and undermined the political credibility of Tyrconnell, his principal Irish supporter. The Jacobite army could neither understand nor forgive the leadership that had involved it in such a heavy defeat, particularly when most of the troops had not engaged the enemy at all. For the rest of the war Irish resistance took on a more nationalist character, but in the medium term the Irish Catholics' political options were severely limited. As the *aisling* poems of the eighteenth-century Gaelic poets signify, they had little alternative to tying themselves to the fortunes of the Catholic branch of the house of Stuart and its powerful patron, the king of France.

War and peace

The French brigade returned home after the Boyne. The rest of the Jacobite army rallied to Limerick, where it regrouped and, in August, under better leadership, successfully defended the city against William and maintained the line of the Shannon. In 1691 further assistance came from France. However, Athlone was captured and the Jacobite army routed at the battle of Aughrim in County Galway. Peace followed with the treaty of Limerick, which had the appearance of a compromise but was in reality a Williamite victory that ushered in the era of the penal laws and consolidated Protestant ascendancy in Ireland. The war finally destroyed the old Catholic gentry as a political force; when Irish Catholics reasserted themselves again, more than a century later, it was under very different leadership.

After the Boyne, James II's chance of recovering his lost thrones was remote, and his credibility everywhere had been greatly undermined. William, in contrast, had consolidated his grip on Britain and Ireland, but the commitment of so much of his military resources to Ireland for three years weakened his offensive capability on the Continent, and to that extent at least the Irish war represented a success for Louis XIV that he obtained for a comparatively modest investment of French troops and resources. There was also the additional gain of battle-hardened Irish soldiers after the war in Ireland ended, when the larger part of the Jacobite army, like its Williamite counterpart, was shipped to the Continent and participated in the continuing war between Louis and the Grand Alliance, until the treaty of Ryswick ended hostilities in 1697.

The 'Wild Geese' – migrant Irish soldiers with roots in the Jacobite army – were to be found not only in France but in the armies of many European states throughout the eighteenth century. In the nineteenth century the deeds of the Jacobite soldiers at home and abroad formed an important strand of Thomas Davis's concept of an historic Irish nation. Most of William's Ulster regiments were demobilised, but three were permanently retained in the British army and laid the foundation of an Anglo-Irish military tradition that endured to modern times.

Commemorating the battle

A tall obelisk, with suitable inscriptions to commemorate the Williamite victory, was erected in 1736 beside Oldbridge ford 'by the grateful contributions of several Protestants of Great Britain and Ireland'. It was destroyed by an explosion in 1923, but a portion of the base may still be seen on an outcrop of rock on the north bank, beside the modern iron bridge. An equestrian statue of William III in College Green, Dublin, erected in 1701, survived several explosions, but was eventually blown up in 1929.

On the tercentenary of the Boyne, in 1990, a modern statue of William was erected at Carrickfergus, where he had first come ashore in Ireland. As a 'Protestant triumph', the Boyne is commemorated annually in Northern Ireland and in parts of Scotland and Canada. This tradition dates back to the eighteenth century and became especially strong from the 1790s on, following the establishment of the Orange Order. This organisation takes its name

The obelisk erected to commemorate the battle

from William's secondary title, prince of Orange, which derived from the small, independent state on the Rhône that was ruled by his family until its seizure by Louis XIV in 1660, and subsequent incorporation into France.

Further reading

Demetrius Charles Boulger, *The battle of the Boyne* (London, 1911).

Peter Berresford Ellis, *The Boyne water* (London, 1976).

Kenneth Ferguson, 'The organisation of King William's army in Ireland 1689–92' in *The Irish Sword*, vol. xviii, no. 70 (winter 1990), pp 62–79.

Peter Harrington, 'Images of the Boyne' in *The Irish Sword*, vol. xviii, no. 70 (winter 1990), pp 57–61.

G.A Hayes-McCoy, *Irish battles* (London, 1969), especially pp 214–72.

Jaqueline R. Hill, 'National festivals, the state and "protestant ascendancy" in Ireland, 1790-1829' in *Irish Historical Studies*, vol. xxiv, no. 93 (May 1984), pp 30–51.

Pádraig Lenihan, *1690 battle of the Boyne* (Stroud, 2003).

Michael McNally, *Battle of the Boyne 1690: the Irish campaign for the English crown* (Osprey, 2005).

W.A. Maguire (ed.), *Kings in conflict: the revolutionary war in Ireland and its aftermath* (Belfast, 1990).

Sheila Mulloy, 'French eye-witnesses of the Boyne' in *The Irish Sword*, vol. xv, no. 59 (winter 1982), pp 104–11.

Diarmuid and Harman Murtagh, 'The Irish Jacobite army' in *The Irish Sword*, vol. xviii, no. 70 (winter 1990), pp 32–48.

Donal O'Carroll, 'An indifferent good post: the battlefield of the Boyne' in *The Irish Sword*, vol. xviii, no. 70 (winter 1990), pp 49–56.

Rober Shepherd, Ireland's Fate: The Boyne and After (London, 1990).

J.G. Simms, 'Eye-witnesses of the Boyne' in *The Irish Sword*, vol. vi, no. 22 (summer 1963), pp 16–27.

J.G. Simms, *Jacobite Ireland 1685-91* (London, Toronto, 1969).

The Boyne Valley Honey company
has published other books on Irish heritage
written by expert authors.
Our website gives full details, but here is an
overview of the publications which
may be of interest…

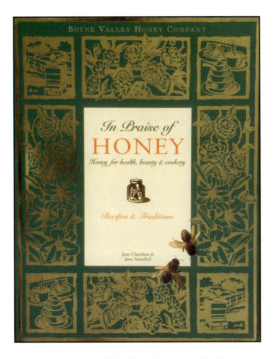

In Praise of Honey: Honey for Health, Beauty & Cookery
Jane Charlton & Jane Newdick

A wealth of intriguing anecdotes, memorable quotations and curious facts along with a fascinating honey survey. This book examines honey's long journey, tracing the journey from bee to honey pot and its place in legend and lore, art and literature. It shows just why honey has endured for so long as a symbol of well-being and health.

There is also a mouth-watering range of tempting honey recipes and treats, from scrumptious cakes, biscuits, sweets and deserts to delicious snacks and starters, main courses, salads and vegetables. Also included is a tasting chart of honeys from around the world so you can refine your tastebuds and become a honey connoisseur. For those who don't like cooking, there are plenty of recipes for honey-based natural remedies and beauty preparations too.

Illustrated throughout with historical pictures, honey memorabilia and striking colour photographs, *In Praise of Honey* is a gorgeous celebration of one of the world's favourite foods.

www.boynevalleyhoney.com

Irish High Crosses
(With the figure sculptures explained)
Peter Harbison

High Crosses are among the most important monuments to survive from Ireland's Golden Age of Saints and Scholars, and over seventy-five of them are described in detail here. Their figure carvings illustrate scenes from the Bible, and this guide explains what the individual panels represent. Many novel identifications offered by the author shed new light on the deeper religious messages of the crosses, which can vary according to the choice of biblical subjects. The book is designed as a field guide for those who want to study the crosses at first-hand, and numerous diagrams assist in pinpointing the various Old and New Testament scenes sculpted on them.

The crosses are arranged in the alphabetical order of their sites, and a map and national grid references should help the reader to locate them on the ground.

Peter Harbison is one of the foremost experts on Irish art and archaeology.

www.boynevalleyhoney.com

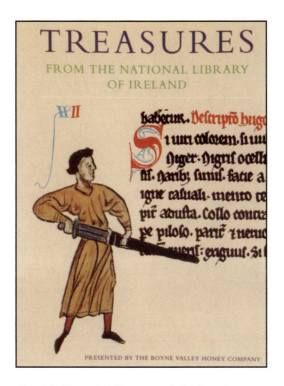

Treasures from the National Library of Ireland
Edited by Noel Kissane

The National Library of Ireland is a major repository of literary and cultural heritage. It holds close to one million books and extensive collections of news-papers, drawings and photographs. In addition, The Genealogical Office, which is linked to the NLI, holds the records of the former Office of Arms (established in 1552). The 100 treasures featured in this selection are from the four corners of Ireland, from Britain, continental Europe, the United States and Australia, and are now preserved for posterity in the collections of the National Library. They represent over 1,000 years of Irish history and cultural achievement at home and overseas.

The book was written by members of National Library's expert staff. Each of the 100 treasures is described and set in context by the curator who is the authority on the collection from which it is drawn.

Also available in Irish: *Seoda I Leabharlann nÁisiunta na hÉireann*

www.boynevalleyhoney.com

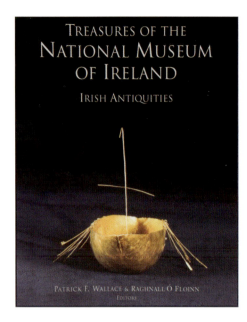

Treasures of the National Museum of Ireland

Edited by Patrick F. Wallace and Raghnall Ó Floinn

This magnificent book, lavishly illustrated with almost 250 full-colour photographs, is a comprehensive introduction to the Irish antiquities collection of the National Museum of Ireland.

The Museum's collections include some of the most important Celtic and pre-Celtic artefacts in the world. Treasures of the National Museum of Ireland selects the highlights: over 200 artefacts are illustrated, described and discussed, including such world-famous objects as the Broighter Boat, the Ardagh Chalice, the Tara Brooch and the Cross of Cong.

Ranging in date from 4500BC to AD1500, the objects described here include the Museum's significant collections of Bronze Age gold, Early Christian jewellery and altar vessels, culminating in church treasures of the later Middle Ages. The illustrated objects are fully captioned and are accompanied by explanatory essays covering each major period, written by members of the Museum's staff.

This is the most comprehensive and authoritative general work yet on the National Museum of Ireland's antiquities collection and should establish itself as the standard guide for many years to come.

www.boynevalleyhoney.com

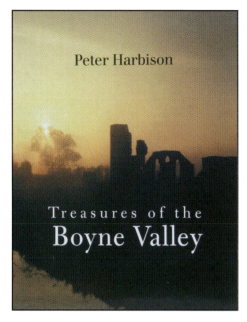

Treasures of the Boyne Valley
Peter Harbison

Peter Harbison's beautiful full-colour book traces the course of the Boyne river from source to sea, detailing its history, the landscape, the peoples who have left their imprint on the region since pre-historic times, the houses and monuments, the battle sites, and all the other aspects that make the Boyne Valley a unique heritage site.

The highlight of the book is the imposing trio of megalithic burial sites at Dowth, Knowth and Newgrange – all at least as old as the Egyptian pyramids. The premier tourist site of Newgrange has been named one of the Wonders of Europe.

Peter Harbison also describes the houses, churches and monastic settlements scattered across the landscape and examines other events and periods that marked the Boyne Valley, such as the Battle of the Boyne (1690), a watershed in Irish history. He also provides an account of the many writers who lived in the region, like Mary Lavin, Francis Ledwidge and Lord Dunsany, whose writings evoke the beauty and tranquillity of the Boyne Valley.

The book is richly illustrated with original landscape photographs by Tom Kelly – himself a resident of the valley – and with historic prints and water-colours. It is the perfect souvenir or gift for anyone who has visited and been seduced by the Boyne Valley.

And for the younger readers...

The Battle of the Boyne 1690: The Drummer Boy's Story

Brenda Maguire

This is the story of the Battle of the Boyne brought to life for the younger reader. It is the story of David and Steph, who witness the Battle of the Boyne at first-hand.

David Peavoy is twelve years old, but he is old enough to enlist as a drummer in the Jacobite army and seek his fortune in a battle campaign. When he meets Stephen Mahon, a young boy from the Liberties in Dublin, he learns a very surprising secret — and makes a friend for life.

Together, David and Stephen embark on an adventure that will change their lives: they join King James' ranks for the greatest battle ever fought on Irish soil. Along with 25,000 soldiers, generals and officers, they face King William and his 36,000-strong army. Both kings are determined to win because the Crown of England and Ireland is at stake. Who will emerge victorious, and who will be defeated?

A story of war, friendship and history in the making.

www.boynevalleyhoney.com

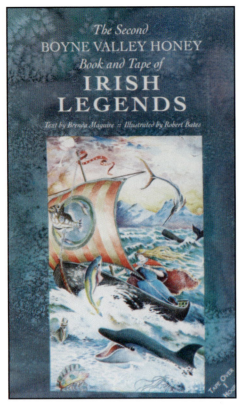

Irish Legends (Book and Tape)

Text by Brenda Maguire

Illustrated by Robert Bates

This book is an anthology of unforgettable stories from the Irish tradition. The stories it recounts were first told thousands of years ago, so long ago we've forgotten who wrote them or when they were written. They were told by storytellers at fairs and firesides, and later by grandmothers and fathers, uncles and sisters. The oldest people in the village told them to the youngest and that was how they survived, being passed down from person to person.

This book brings to life six stories from the myths and legends of ancient Ireland. These are tales that have been told for centuries, now gathered together and delightfully retold by Brenda Maguire and superbly illustrated by Robert Bates.

The accompanying tape features the voices of Kathleen Watkins, Niall Toibin, Ronnie Drew, Paul Acheson, Maxi and Marian Finucane: a perfect cast to animate these stories for young listeners.

This book is also available in Irish: *Finnscéalta na hÉireann.*

P.T.O $\longrightarrow$ CD + MAP

P.T.O $\longrightarrow$